ROSARIES
from the Hearts of Jesus and Mary

as given to
Rita Ring

Shepherds of Christ Publications
Madison, Indiana

In conformity with the decrees of Pope Urban VIII, the Publisher recognizes and accepts that the final authority regarding all messages rests with the Holy See of Rome, to whose judgment we willingly submit.

—*The Publisher*

This book is published by Shepherds of Christ Publications, a subsidiary of Shepherds of Christ Ministries, a tax exempt religious public charitable corporation organized to foster devotion to the Two Hearts, the Sacred Heart of Jesus and the Immaculate Heart of Mary. Messages were given at Our Lady of the Holy Spirit Center, Norwood, Ohio to Rita Ring, Marty Coby and the Ring children, Cathy and Joseph Ring. Messages were transcribed from tape by Marty Coby. Spiritual consultant was Father Edward J. Carter, S.J., spiritual advisor of Shepherds of Christ Ministries. Design: Larry Memering. Front cover artwork is by Harold Kellner, Sidney, Ohio. Title page photo is of Sorrowful Mother Statue, Our Lady of the Holy Spirit Center, Norwood, Ohio.

Internet: http://www.shepherds-of-christ.org

For additional copies, write to:
Shepherds of Christ Ministries
P.O. Box 193
Morrow, Ohio 45152-0193
Toll Free 1-888-211-3041
          (513) 932-4451

Biblical quotations have been taken from *The New Jerusalem Bible*, Doubleday, New York, N.Y., 1990.

First Printing: December, 1996
Second Printing, April, 1997
Third Printing: August, 1998

DEDICATION

To the Hearts of Jesus and Mary
and to Father Edward Carter, S.J.

IN APPRECIATION

I want to thank Jesus and Mary for these rosaries from
Their Hearts for this world.

Special thanks to:

St. Michael for helping us to publish this book.

Fr. Edward Carter S.J. for attending the rosaries, putting
in many hours of service, discerning these rosaries, and for
his endless support and spiritual direction.

Harold Kellner for his artwork and videotaping. I thank
Harold and his wife for their support.

I want to thank Cathy and Joe Ring for attending all the
rosaries daily during the fourteen months and Cathy for all
her help with the publication of the rosaries.

Joe Lee for all his work in formating this music for publication. Mary has asked Joe to do this. It is a great contribu-
tion to this book.

Carol Kissinger, Ellen Sartori and Emily Lehrter for
their secretarial assistance.

Chris Finkbone, Mike and Brian Arlinghaus for their
help.

Tom Arlinghaus for his great friendship and support.

John Weickert, president, who has supported me and
helped me to circulate the rosary aves to the schools.

Mary Rettig as school rosary coordinator.

And lastly, I'd like to thank my dear uncle Andrew Weber.

CONTENTS

CONTENTS
– *Continued* –

BACKGROUND

The Rosary

The Rosary gives us a chance to experience Their life, to feel it, to let it become a part of us. We empty our minds of all that is happening and live the mysteries with Jesus and Mary. We experience the emotions with Them. They tap into our hearts as we experience some of the emotions of the Hearts of Jesus and Mary–a parade of emotions, a reliving in our hearts, a sharing of feelings with Jesus and Mary.

These are Rosaries from the Hearts of Jesus and Mary. It takes time to pray the rosary. It gives us a time to put our world aside and be there in Their lives. His life was given for love of us. I am called by Mary to lead others to the love of Her precious Son. When I carry out His life in my life, then I will preach the Gospel in my life.

Do I act as Christ did? Let us look at our lives and see if we are acting like Him today. We live Their lives in the rosary.

How the Rosary Meditations Began
at Our Lady of the Holy Spirit Center

The message below is from June 16, 1994. When I received this message, there appeared little sparkling lights on my notebook, lights that are like the lights I saw surrounding Mary. I received this message at 3:15 a.m.

Jesus: Soon your burden will be lifted and you will feel some relief. You must be in constant prayer. Being with your children is a prayer for you. Come to Our Lady of the Holy Spirit Center. You feel the Real Presence there. I will give you miracles there. Pray in the chapel with your children. They will become closer to Me through prayer as you spend time praying with them. You need simplicity in your life. Live only for love of Me.

Note: Little white lights on my notebook.

An Explanation of What Is to Follow

Jesus and Mary give me little insights into the Father's plan, little pieces of the puzzle. They do not tell everything that will happen. In order to understand the plan, we need to study all the messages and see how the Father's plan is unfolding. We are all threads of the great tapestry, all little puzzle pieces of the big picture, all so important to His plan.

We are all being called to spread His love to this world. Each soul is so important to His plan. I see now many events as they unfold. I see where Jesus and Mary told me many things and I at the time did not understand. I was told in June that I would see as never before.

On July 4, 1994 I prayed with the children in front of the Our Lady of Grace statue in the sanctuary. On July 5, I recorded our experiences. The statue of Mary continued to glow and come alive. Jesus and Mary told Fr. Carter to pray with the children and me on July 10.

I would see Mary glow. Several weeks later I realized she was appearing in the statue as "Our Lady of Light." She then began to say she was appearing as "Our Lady of Light." She would show me a parade of faces, her clothes would all turn glistening white, and her attire would change. She would appear as a parade of different ladies. Her veils and head coverings would change. She has appeared as many different Marys. Her emotions have varied, her age has varied and her clothing has varied. She has shown me her life in the rosary. In the rosary, we meditate on the lives of Jesus and Mary, from Their young lives to Their older lives, from Their sorrows to Their joys. She takes on many roles as our mother, her mantle forever covering and protecting us.

July 5, 1994 6:30 p.m.

I was told to go to Our Lady of the Holy Spirit Center to pray the rosary with my children. There were people in the front of the church, so we decided to pray the rosary in the back before the Sorrowful Mother statue. I had the following vision at the end of the rosary.

The statue of the Sorrowful Mother was lit up as if she had fire around her. The light was very bright. Her whole gown was all-white, but the statue's gown is blue and pink. She was all aglow. It looked like the glow that comes off of a fire. Her face kept changing but remained totally sorrowful–the sorrow of an older woman. She was in such pain and sorrow! (It was hard to explain how she looked–extremely pained!) Her face looked as though she was in such pain that she could hardly bear it.

The vision remained like this for about ten minutes, having begun during the last Hail Mary of the Sorrowful Mysteries of the rosary. She was holding something–it was all bright white–the brightest light ever!

– From Blue Book IV

July 6, 1994 6:30 p.m.

Vision (in front of the Sorrowful Mother statue): I was told by Mary to go alone at 6:30 p.m. to Our Lady of the Holy Spirit Center. I prayed the Sorrowful Mysteries again, saying a sentence at each Hail Mary. She was aglow, all in white. She remained like this for at least 10 minutes.

July 9, 1994 6:30 p.m.

Vision: I was going to Dayton to a party. I stopped at the Center around 6:25 p.m. and prayed the Sorrowful Mysteries with my children. I prayed on each bead. Toward the end of the third mystery, Mary's statue became illuminated. Her face was brilliant, so bright! Her gown was white. Her face was beautiful! I could hardly talk for the next two mysteries. She stayed like this for a long time afterwards.

Explanation of Rosary Meditations and Visions

On July 10, Jesus and Mary told Fr. Carter to go to Our Lady of the Holy Spirit Center and pray the rosary with my children and me. He came to the Center every day and led the rosary. Mary told me to say a meditation on every bead.

On July 14, I prayed a meditation on every bead as Fr. Carter led the rosary. During the middle of the fifth mystery, Mary started to change faces. I saw all different expressions, all different ages–older, sorrowful, young, beautiful, mostly joyful. The faces would first be old, then young. Lights would flash on and off.

There was a constant shadow of the cross, with Christ on it, behind the statue of Our Lady. The veil around her head would change from bright whites to darker shades. Her head cover would change with her many faces. I was so weak that I could hardly move the chair when the rosary was over. I felt totally exhausted.

Father Carter continued to pray the rosary every day with us for about 3 1/2 months. Jesus and Mary told him to come and pray. We were taught more and more about the lives of Jesus and Mary through the rosary.

In October of 1994, as Father Carter became more involved in Shepherds of Christ Ministries, Jesus and Mary told him to make his holy hour at his residence. Mary sent Marty Coby and told me that she was my rosary partner and that Father Carter was asked to help us with the rosary.

On October 31, the day before All Saints Day, Marty, Gerry Ross and I prayed before Mary's statue in the grotto at the Center. We saw visions for two hours after praying the rosary. Marty and I saw a parade of saints, and the statue of Mary turned into Jesus for a very long time. It was so beautiful! It was as if we were watching a movie. We both saw the same thing.

The rosary meditations for October 31 follow below. It is very significant that this was the beginning of the published rosary meditations and that Marty, Gerry and I were present. Mary's statue changing into Jesus' image shows the intimacy between Their lives and the beginning of the rosaries from the Hearts of Jesus and Mary. Marty was asked by Mary to sing the Ave Maria before each rosary. Now we have included the song Our Lady of Fatima at the end. Marty and I continued to visit Our Lady of the Holy Spirit Center every day until September of 1995. Our last rosary prayed there was September 5, 1995 and on a video (from that day) we saw the Sorrowful Mother statue surrounded by a pink mist. Marty and I saw visions every day as Mary came alive in the statue and the pictures of Jesus became lifelike. Marty received many visions while typing the rosaries. Her labors of love are given here, as she taped and transcribed all these rosaries from the Hearts of Jesus and Mary to you.

July 12, 1994 1:49 a.m.

Jesus: I am the Way. I am the Truth. I am the Light of Life. My candle is a candle that shines bright in the darkest night for love of all. I shine with warmth and joy and love for you. Come in the night. I miss you, every day. Continue to pray the rosary at 6:30 at the Center. No questions asked. The gifts of God have unfolded upon you.

July 14, 1994

The rosary tells of the lives of Christ and Mary. How can I be Christ-like if I do not meditate on His life? My life is to be a model of Christ's life. How can I model myself after how He loved if I am not intimately involved in a love relationship with Him?

Christ shows us the way. His passion and death have meaning in that He did it for our salvation and for love of us. The more I meditate on the rosary, the more I see the oneness of Christ and His Mother. They shared each other's pains, sorrows, joys, suffering. They were so connected to each other! This is shown all through the passion, her sorrows, the presentation of Jesus in the Temple, the finding of Jesus in the Temple, her journey into Egypt, her journey during the passion when Their eyes met (this alone could be meditated on to tell of their union and their suffering), watching the putting of nails in His hands, standing under the cross, beholding His lifeless body under the cross after His death, laying Him in the tomb.

Their Hearts beat as one as she suffered silently with Him. No mother was ever so connected with her son as was Mary. Sorrow increases intimacy when I suffer in union with Christ. I am admitting how much He is truly a Person I depend on. I want to depend on Him completely. I want to be so close to Him that it is He to whom I run when my heart is torn. He loves us so. He knows our every thought and feeling. He loves us with such attentiveness and care and He waits for us to run to His arms and share ourselves with Him.

He longs for our love. He longs for our time. He wants us to go to Him as our best friend, a real Person. But what a Person, and what He can do for us! You are My Savior, Lord. You saved me from my sins by Your brutal death. You give me life in Your resurrection. I am born into Your life in baptism and You live in my heart. God lives in me! Father, Son and Holy Spirit dwell within my breast, and Mary is so united to Jesus!

Oh, God, I love you so. I want to know You and love You and serve You. Spirit, open me to know my precious Lord. I am Yours to possess and I live to do Your holy Will. Father, fashion me, mold me more into the image of Jesus, Your precious Son, so that Christ lives in me more and more. I want to be one in You, through Him, with Him and in Him.

Meditating on the rosary is meditating on Christ's life. How can I be molded more into His image if I do not meditate on Him and His life?

The first commandment demands that I love God above all things. What is love? Is it lip service, or is it a fire that burns within your soul? May my heart burn in deepest love of God—Father, Son and Holy Spirit. May I grow in intimacy with each Person and with Mary.

Jesus died that we all might live. He shed the last drop of His blood for us. He gave the last beat of His Heart for each and every person. Help us to unite as brothers in Christ.

August 1, 1994

The following is the first official message I received before the statue of Mary at Our Lady of the Holy Spirit Center. It is a personal message for Father Carter.

Mary (in front of the glowing statue of Our Lady of Sorrows): I am the Immaculate Heart. My Heart is glowing for love of all my beloved children. I am your most loving Mother. I am with you this day. Pray for the success of the priestly newsletter *Shepherds of Christ.* I am guarding your way. You will receive such graces to accomplish this task! Grace from God is so abundantly bestowed on you and will lead to the success of this endeavor! Pray for this cause at the Center. The priests will lead the people to the love of My beloved Son. This is no little task. It will take many prayers and graces. Pray hard, little one. Your prayers will change many hearts.

I am Mary, your Immaculate Mother. I bring this message to My beloved priest-son.

August 10, 1994 After Mass, Fr. Smith's Chapel

See Mary as she beholds the baby in her arms. She looks at

Him so tenderly. His sweet baby eyes look up at the eyes of His loving Mother. Such tenderness between Mother and Son, such oneness to hold her infant Son so lovingly in her arms. Oh, do we ever know the tenderness between a baby and his loving mother?

A life of close union between this mother and this Son, a life of her looking into His loving eyes. Such silent, but strong and loving communication! Such a strong bond–their eyes meeting–from one soul to the other soul.

Song: See the eyes that look at Mary (Verse 1)…

Deep, deep communication, a deep bond, indescribable in words, a touching of the souls! And the peering look between Son and mother on the road to the crucifixion. What a peering look, what communication between this Son and Mother. Seeing the other suffer was as agonizing as each's very own suffering–suffering and oneness between a Son and His mother. A peering look, deep into the very souls. Such an intimacy between Them!

How can one describe in words this oneness, this union between the Son and His Mother? The perfect love between Him and her. Total giving of each person in such love to the other. To see the suffering of the other was as agonizing as–if not more than– each's own suffering.

How His passion and crucifixion were intensified by the sufferings of His dear Mother! How her sufferings were such a sharing in our redemption, the swords that pierced her Heart! The eyes of Mary that invisibly bled as she watched such brutality to the beloved baby she once carried in her womb and held in her arms!

Song: Little baby hands and feet…

Mary held the Child Jesus when he was a baby; she watched Him and cared for Him as a little boy; she was so attentive to the needs of her little Son. Will we ever know this connectedness between Their loving hearts? Do we know this oneness? The peering eyes on the way to Calvary tell the story. They tell the story of this oneness. They tell the story of her watching this horrid event of her beautiful baby Son and His horrible passion and death.

Her eyes! Oh, Mary, help me to see the love of Jesus through your eyes! You watched Him as a baby, you watched Him as a child. You watched Him grow into the beautiful man He became and you, Mary, watched Him all through this bitter passion and death. Your eyes saw the love that He gave for us. Now you come, Mary. You appear to tell us to go to this Son. You knew more than anyone His love to suffer so for us. You come and appear with blood in your eyes and tears running down your cheeks. You show me your sorrowful face, your young face, your old face, your joyful face. This was the face Jesus peered at as He walked His walk to Calvary. This was the face that appears now to tell us the story of His love this very day. I see your parade of faces, Mary, old and young, sorrowful and joyful. I see these faces that Jesus beheld. Your face tells the story of His love for us.

Mary: This is my beloved Son. This is my baby. This is the child I bore in my womb. He came to give you love. He came to be God-made-Man among you this very day. He is, my children, no less present in the Eucharist than He was at Calvary and you go after such incidental things. My Son loves you. I show you my face so you can tell the world of our love. Live our lives in the rosary. Let our lives live in your day. The way to eternal happiness is to be likened to my beautiful Son.

I watched my Son. I lead you to the ardent love of my Son, Jesus. His Heart burns for love of you. Come to Him this day. Give Him your love. Spend time with Him. He is alive and in your midst in the Eucharist.

Note: I smelled roses very strongly throughout this message.

Song: See the eyes that look at Mary (Verse 2)…

R. This is the Son of the Father, the Son of God, born of Mary through the Holy Spirit, and He lives this day in your hearts. Share His love for you. Go to Him through Mary's Heart. She who is so closely united to Jesus! Their hearts are so close to one another! As their eyes were joined in such oneness, their hearts are joined in such intimacy. Go to Jesus' Heart through His beloved Mother, through her who bore Him in her womb, her who watched Him give Himself for love of you.

August 11, 1994

Jesus: Oh, how I watched you, child. I watched you as I gave you each little sign of My love. I watched you grow in your faith and trust in Me. I watched you suffer and stood so close you could have touched Me, but you didn't know that this suffering would be that which led you to My tender love for you.

I watched you when you surrendered and turned your will over to Me and I watched you cry, knowing this was the most joyous day of your life. I watched you see visions of doors and knew you would want to go through those doors, but they were not the doors you thought, they were the doors I gave you for greater union with Me. I watched you, child, when you wrote down My first letter to you and I saw your confusion and joy, knowing what these letters would do to touch so many hearts.

I watched you, child. I watched you when I showed you My Heart and you were so warmed by this Heart and so awed by its vision, but you didn't know what this vision would mean for many to draw their hearts to My burning love.

I watched you surrender each time as you let go of each little thing, as you were dying to self. I watched you through this surrender grow closer to Me. I watched you grow in this deep love for Me, step by step. I watched our love grow as you gave more of yourself in prayer. I watched you, child, and I loved being ever closer to you.

I watched you struggle in such trials that you thought tomorrow would never come, knowing that this trial was what would give you more freedom and love for Me. I watched you learn each lesson through hard tests and I was so close while you struggled, but did not remove the struggle, knowing you would not learn your lesson if I had.

I watched you, child, through each joy and pain and I loved you silently, always with you, and you never knew how close I truly was to you.

Song: From the day you were born…

From the day you were born, I watched you. Forever by your side, I guarded you, I loved you. I know the most secret desire of your heart far better than you yourself know. I know the Father's plan for you. I know the Father's love for you. I know the love poured on you from the Holy Spirit and how Mary is forever by your side.

I watch you, child, constantly guarding you and your ways and you do not know the love I have for you. You do not know how My Heart burns for love of you. And, someday, My beautiful child, you will know what I have in store for you, My beloved. Come and be with Me. Grow in your love with Me. I never leave you, My beloved. Remember, I am forever watching you.

August 18, 1994

Vision: I see her hold His lifeless body under the cross. I see her tenderness, holding Him as a baby. I see their oneness in the peering eyes. I see her with the sword in her Heart, pierced from her sharing in the sufferings of her Son. I see her giving birth to her beautiful baby.

I see her sorrowful face, her beautiful face, her old face, her young face, all reflections of her life and His life. Joined in joy, joined in suffering, joined—mother and Son—throughout the life, death and resurrection of Jesus. They want us to live in Their Hearts today.

August 23, 1994

R. The bond between Jesus and Mary started when He was conceived. The bond between a mother and son or daughter is so strong because the child grows within the mother's womb.

Mary: I felt His life within my very body. This connection between myself and my Son began from the first moment of conception. For nine months I carried the Son of God growing within me. What joy, what honor, to carry the child Jesus within my womb! The Spirit filled my being constantly.

Carry His life within your being. Jesus wants to be alive in your very heart. The Spirit wants to be a force alive in your heart. The Spirit wants to permeate your very being and make you alive with the fire of God's love. The Father is present in your heart. Your Father loved you and molded you in your mother's womb. He cares for you as no other father ever cared for his child. You are His, created out of love.

You are truly a child of God and my most loved child. I mother you as I mothered my Son Jesus. Oh, little child of mine, turn to me as your most loving mother. Do not try to go it alone. From the love I have for Jesus, I will lead you to His precious Heart. Come to me and let me lead you to such close union with my Son! The Father is my Father, the Spirit my Spouse. Come and let me lead you to the unlimited love of God!

He truly guards you every minute of the day. His love is constant. Jesus is forever a burning furnace on fire for love of you. Come to His Heart through my Immaculate Heart. It is truly the love of Our Two Hearts that will lead you to such union with God!

I am the Immaculate Heart. I am your loving mother. I am here with you this moment. Take my hand and let me lead you to such union with God!

I am your Mother and I thank you for responding to my call.

September 2, 1994 After Communion

R. Such emotion I feel, looking at Mary's statues. I can hardly take it in. I feel so close to Christ in my heart and have an intense longing for Him. I felt a burning in my chest, wanting more. I felt such sorrow around Mary, I couldn't bear to look at the statue and wanted to cry.

Mary: My little girl, I am Mary, your beloved mother. As I have told you, you will suffer. My Heart is so sad for all those who do not know the love of my Son. You know some of His intense love for all the beloved souls. I give you some of my emotions to allow you to experience my suffering, to know all those who reject the love of my precious Son. Sweet child of mine, you know how He loves all. I tell you to pray, pray for each other.

Promote the rosary. I am showing you how to make the rosary alive in your life. The rosary is such a powerful prayer against Satan. Satan is running rampant. He will be squelched by the praying of the rosary. Promote the rosary. I appear to you as the Lady of Light. My rosary will light up the world! I am the Immaculate Heart of Mary. Who will hear if you are not speaking? Constantly be about the work of promoting Our Two Hearts and praying the rosary. I show myself to you to comfort you and to lead others to my rosary. I am sorrowful to know the hearts of men. They have turned so cold, when Jesus has a burning fire waiting to warm them.

Jesus: I am Jesus. I am the Sacred Heart of Jesus. My Heart burns for love of My beloved children. It is through My Mother's Heart and My Heart that so many will turn their cold hearts and lukewarm hearts to hearts ablaze with the fire of My love.

Promote My Heart through My Mother's Heart. You will continue to experience such emotions! My Mother is so closely united to Me! To know her is to know her suffering for the sinners that will be lost in eternal damnation. She appears to you in such light! You must preach the contents of these letters. Your words will be a light to the dark world. I speak through you. You are delivering My messages to those I love. Your tongue should forever declare My intense, burning love for all. This world will shine with the love of My Sacred Heart. These words will illuminate their hearts. You hold words given to My loved ones from Me. Do not take this job lightly. You need to get my messages out. Souls will be lost forever because they did not know My burning love. This is the medicine for the sick world. They need these messages.

I am Jesus. I speak here to the world. These are My intense love letters to all. They need to hear these words. They are given from Me to each precious soul. This is an urgent message. Time is so short! You will know soon that the time delayed will hurt many souls.

Souls will not know of My love. They need these messages. I speak so tenderly to My beloved ones here! Please, I beg you to spread these words to My hurting children.

Mary is appearing as a Lady of Light. These letters will light men's hearts with My intense love for them. The world will shine with My love. Circulate the messages. This is an urgent message.

December 24, 1994

Jesus: My dear little child, please write up the meditations on the rosary. Ask Marty to help you and ask Harold to use his picture for the cover. You are to begin recounting your experiences daily. Start with the experiences from July 5, 1994. Include Fr. Carter's part in the rosary and Marty's part in the rosary. Write down the events you see daily, by date. Write down what you see. Include October 31, 1994 rosary. Marty is your partner in publishing the rosary book. You should list all you both see. Include the Christmas rosary. Begin by writing down your rosary meditations. All will become clear as you begin your rosary journal. Your time recounting these events will lead to a closer understanding of Our lives and Our intimacy with each other.

Mary: Your union with My Son and the Father and the Holy Spirit will deepen as your understanding of the union between myself and Jesus grows. From this day forward you will be closely united to me, your mother, and closely united to Jesus through the rosary. I want you to lead the rosary always. Always dim the lights and use candles. I will be there and Jesus will be there whenever you pray the rosary. We will be with you in a very special way. Your job is to promote the rosary. When you pray the rosary, tell them about my letters to them, centered around my Son in the Eucharist.

Always pray the rosary. Always center it in the Eucharist. Ask Marty and Fr. Carter to help you. This will be a powerful tool for bringing many to the rosary and to loving My Son in the Eucharist. I am Mary, your mother, and that is My Christmas gift to all. Pray the rosary for us.

Mary: My dear ones, I want pictures of the rosary and seven sorrows in the rosary book. I would like meditations on the seven sorrows. I would like the songs that could be used during the different mysteries of the rosary. I would like rosary meditations and certain messages that pertain to meditations on some mysteries. My rosary, prayed as I have instructed, will lead many hearts to Our Two Hearts. We are so closely united in the rosary. The rosary is the most beautiful prayer. Singing between the Hail Marys pleases me so much. Lift up your hearts. Pray the rosary with your whole heart and it will live in your day. I, your beloved mother, and My Son thank you for responding to my call.

August 11, 1995

We are the children of the light. Mary is our Mother. She is the new Eve. Jesus is the new Adam. It is Mary who will lead the precious children to the Heart of her Son. We, the children of the light, are her army marching in battle against the enemy, the devil. He wants to devour all precious souls and take them to hell.

Jesus comes and gives us His life, released through the Heart of His Mother. He came to give us life to the full and take us home with Him.

I hear Him call out, "I am alive, I am alive, I am alive and I live in the hearts of men." As I live in the Hearts of Jesus and Mary, as I unite with Their Hearts, my actions are actions likened to their action. They are living through me in this world. As I model my life after Their Lives, as I dwell in Their Hearts, as I unite with Mary and Jesus, and as I live in Their hearts, I live in peace and joy, according to the Father's Will. As each of us live in their hearts, we live in the same hearts of Jesus and Mary and we are united in this strong bond of love. We become one in Their hearts. As Mary leads all her children home to her Son through her Heart, the Heart of Mary will triumph on this earth and the Sacred Heart of Jesus will reign.

In one of my deepest experiences with Jesus, I heard, very clearly, Him call out, "I am alive, I am alive, I am alive. I love you, I love you, I love you." This sums up the message of Jesus. He loves us with the deepest love and He is alive this day. He is truly present in the tabernacle and He lives in a special way in the hearts of men. Every day Jesus and Mary have been teaching us through their messages and meditations on the rosary. In the rosary we meditate on the lives of Jesus and Mary. From the Emmaus scene the Gospel says of Jesus: "Then, starting with Moses and going through all the prophets, he explained to them the passages throughout the scriptures that were about himself." (Lk 24:27) He told them, with His burning love, about the scriptures, but they did not know it was Jesus. When they realized later that it was Jesus, they said, "Did not our hearts burn within us as he talked to us on the road and explained the scriptures to us?" (Lk 24:32)

The disciples experienced His burning love when Jesus spoke. Jesus and Mary are giving to us the messages this day that He is alive and loves us so much. He speaks to us in these rosary meditations and messages. As Jesus and Mary have told us about their lives in these meditations, Their lives have grown in my life.

I experienced emotions that Jesus allowed me to feel on Ascension Thursday and heard Him call out, I am alive, I am alive, I am alive. I cried for three days from this experience. Jesus calls out to us this day, "I am alive." It is in the quiet moments that we hear these cries. He lives in the busy and noisy world. As we encounter others, He is alive in others. As we grow in our life with Him, we realize His presence that surrounds us.

It is as the disciples on the way to Emmaus, I have heard the scriptures all my life, but when Jesus began to talk to me they came alive and they live in me, deeper and deeper and deeper. Now, every word I read in the scriptures, every word I pray in the Mass, fills my heart more and more with His burning love.

Jesus wants hearts on fire for love of Him. He remains with us truly present in the Blessed Sacrament, longing and thirsting for His precious souls to come to Him.

He is alive. He is the mighty medicine for the sick world. Rosaries from the Hearts of Jesus and Mary are messages and meditations to activate this burning love in our hearts. He is telling us this day of His love, not to replace the scriptures, but to help His life live in us. He tells us His love to enhance all that the church teaches, to make our hearts burn with the great gifts we are given. Jesus truly is present in the Eucharist, in the Scriptures, and the Sacraments. I love the Church. I love the Mass. I love the Priest. I love, love, love, Jesus in the Eucharist. I love Mary, the Saints, the angels, the souls in purgatory. I love my brother. I love more and more because my heart burns with the love of Jesus, alive this day.

He wants us to love Him with our whole heart, our whole soul, our whole being. He wants our hearts to burn with love of Him. As I attend the Mass and become one with Him in the sacrifice to the Father, my heart is burning with love for the Father, Son and Holy Spirit. He wants the priest to love Him so much and celebrate the Holy Sacrifice of the Mass in such oneness with Him, with their hearts burning with love as they say to the Father, "through Him, with Him and in Him", as they elevate the host and say, "This is My Body, this is My Blood." In their whole being, to put on Christ and become one in this great sacrifice to the Father, united in the Holy Spirit, with Mary, our beloved Mother. What great gifts we are given: the Church, the Mass, the Sacraments, the Priest, the Scriptures, the Rosary – are not our hearts burning within us! As we become one in the pure and tender Heart of Mary, as we live and dwell in her Heart, as we love the Father, as Mary loved her beloved Father, through her Heart and we love her Son as Mary loved her dear and precious Son, and love the Holy Spirit as Mary loved her beloved Spouse, as we learn to love through the Heart of our precious beloved Mary, love God as she loved Him, love each other as she loves her precious little children - then, her Heart will live in this world through us. As we dwell in the Heart of Mary, we dwell in the Heart of Jesus, for she dwells there in deepest union.

Oh, my heart sings as I sing the songs He has given to us. "Oh, burning heart, oh love divine, how dear you are to me. I see the Host, I know you are here to love and care for me. I know your love a little now, how dear you are to me - Come, give me life, abundant life, I thirst to be with thee! " How our life will grow as I give my all to the Father, with Jesus, in the Mass and as I live in the

Hearts of Jesus and Mary and operate with their life flowing from me in this world. How our life will grow as I dwell in their hearts and I am saturated with this life flowing from the pierced Heart of Jesus and the pierced Heart of Mary. My heart is bathed in Their love and Their life. The Holy Spirit will transform me more and more into the image and likeness of Jesus as His Spirit moves in the Heart of Mary and I will be led to a closer union with my beloved Father. Oh burning Heart, my heart burns for love of you. As you pray these rosaries and read these letters from Jesus, may you know more and more His life within you and may your hearts burn in deepest love for Him. I love you, Jesus.

"Come give me life, abundant life, I thirst to be with thee."

A Final Explanation from Rita Ring

Mary appeared almost every day from July 5, 1994 until September 5, 1995 at Our Lady of the Holy Spirit Center. A video taken at the last rosary revealed a pink mist over the statue during key meditations during the rosary. This video is available upon request. Also available are audio tapes of some rosaries in this book and live rosaries received later. A live rosary is a rosary in which I receive these messages directly from Jesus and Mary. Most rosaries last about one hour. They are taped and these meditations and messages are transcribed from this tape. Mary continues to appear to me.

Jesus and Mary have requested that members of the Shepherds of Christ chapters come together on the 13th of each month at 12:00 noon. Jesus has stressed the importance of these rosaries for the completion of the Fatima message. He promises to give His directions to His chosen apostles on that day. Live recordings of these messages given on the 13th are available on tape and in written form.

We still have special rosaries on the fifth of each month. We also receive a special rosary during the weekly Shepherds of Christ meetings. Presently these rosaries are held at Tom Arlinghaus's Farm in Kentucky. The rosary is led by Fr. Carter, messages and meditations are received by Rita Ring, discerned by Fr. Carter, and published by Shepherds of Christ Publications. Jesus and Mary have allowed me on some occasions to travel and deliver messages during the rosary. Only when They advise me to do so do I travel and deliver a special rosary. For any further information concerning audio or video tapes, contact Shepherds of Christ Publications. Mary and Jesus have requested that you help circulate these rosaries. Rosaries without messages and with the Imprimatur are available for children. Mary has requested that we circulate these rosaries and a simple consecration to Jesus and Mary to the children in schools. Both the rosaries and consecrations have the Imprimatur. Will you help to comply to Mary's request and circulate these rosaries and consecrations to children? Will you be a special apostle and answer both Jesus and Mary's request and circulate these rosaries to as many people as possible? These rosaries are a great gift to you from the Hearts of Jesus and Mary. There are many more available. Check our website on the Internet:

http://www.shepherds-of-christ.org

Message from Mary October 1, 1995
Mary: My dear child, please include in the rosary book the message of September 5, 1995 during the pink mist. Also make available an audio tape with this message dated October 1, 1995 and a video of the mist. Please include the remarks given during the mist.

I am Mary, your Mother. Thank you for leading souls to the Eucharistic Heart of My Son.

September 5, 1995
Song: Oh Burning Heart, Oh Love divine, how sweet You are to me. I see the host, I know You're here to love and care for me.

1. Response: Be with Jesus in the Garden of Gethsemane, kneel beside Him, see the rocks, see His brown hair and His beautiful face. This is Jesus Christ, the Son of God. Be there and feel His presence and as you feel His presence, realize the presence of the Almighty God within your hearts: Father, Son and Holy Spirit. At this moment you are surrounded by Their Divine Love and your heart is burning within you as you kneel beside the Almighty God.

2. Response: We do not realize how close He truly is to us, that He wants to be one with us, through Him, with Him, and in Him, that He calls us to this union, to this oneness with Him. As we meditate on the mysteries of this rosary, let us unite in this oneness with the Almighty God who cries from every tabernacle in this world—

cries out deep cries of His burning love and they fall on deaf ears—
who comes to us and gives us Himself in the Holy Eucharist and is
ignored and forgotten and treated with such indifference.

3. Response: Jesus Christ, the Son of God, who waits in all the
tabernacles of the world in the Sacrament of Greatest Love, waiting
a prisoner for His beloved souls to come and to be with Him. As
present as the day that He knelt in the garden, in His divinity and
His humanity, He waits in the tabernacle and we kneel before Him
in front of the tabernacle, as we imagine that we knelt next to Him
in the garden. This is the love that the Almighty God has for us. He
remains with us this day and is forgotten and ignored. He calls out
to His beloved souls, "Come to Me, you are blind and you are deaf,
you do not know the great gifts that you are given. I am waiting and
waiting for you to come. Come to Me, My beloved souls, I long and
thirst to unite in deepest union with you."

We search this barren desert for things to fill our starved soul,
when nothing on the face of the earth will fill the starved soul but
the love of God and He is waiting and longing and thirsting for us
to come and to be with Him.

Oh, beloved Jesus, truly present in the tabernacle, give us the
grace to realize this great gift we are given, to cherish every single
moment that we are in the presence of the Almighty God, to never
take this for granted, to thank You endlessly for the great gift You
have given to us, the gift of Yourself, that You are truly present, the
gift that You give us in the Holy Eucharist, and Your Heart was in
such anguish in the garden, Your Heart of deepest love for all the
souls that would treat You with such indifference and negligence.
Your Heart of burning love is so often ignored and forgotten. My
precious One, let me help make reparation to Your adorable Heart
for all that You suffered in the garden for Your beloved souls who
have forgotten You.

Song: Oh Burning Heart, Oh Love divine, how sweet You are to me.
I see the host, I know You're here to love and care for me.

ROSARY CHAPEL WINDOWS

Importance of the Windows

The Father has a plan for each one of us. He intends us to love God with our whole heart, our whole soul, our whole being. Each person is an important thread in the tapestry in the work of the salvation of mankind.

The Father gives us special gifts and talents and loves us, His precious creations. Jesus loves us so much He gave His life for us!

The Rosary is the lives of Jesus and Mary, their love for us.

The Rosary Chapel at Our Lady of the Holy Spirit Chapel in Norwood, Ohio is part of His plan for the salvation of mankind. I received most of the rosaries at Our Lady of the Holy Spirit Center. Jesus told me the windows were part of His plan. As I sat in the Rosary Chapel, Jesus revealed many insights into the mysteries of His life and His Mother's life. These mysteries will be revealed in more detail in future volumes. As requested by Jesus, pictures of these windows are included here. As you meditate on the mysteries of the Rosary, the lives of Jesus and Mary will come alive in your hearts.

The Rosary Chapel and the windows give me such joy. I see their lives, alive, in these windows. Jesus said many miracles will happen in this chapel when he is in the tabernacle and we pray the rosary there. I love the rosary so much. I love Jesus and Mary, and I thank them for this great gift from their hearts.

November 5, 1996
Before the Exposed Eucharist
Jesus told me He wanted this explanation in the Rosary Book.

19

The Father has told me that His plan will unfold despite all resistance. We are to carry out the life, death and resurrection of Jesus in our lives. We must meditate on the lives of Jesus and Mary to live His life.

It will become so difficult before the era of peace. One way that we will stay focused on Him is to meditate on His life as we pray the rosary.

Mary told St. Dominic that the rosary and the scapular will be great instruments in the salvation of the world.

Satan presses on our minds. We must discipline our thoughts. We must focus on God and not give into Satan who is constantly trying to torment our minds.

This is why Mary has asked us to pray three rosaries a day. We are constantly, all through the day, turning our thoughts to the mysteries of their lives. It is hard to get the three rosaries in, but by praying them, we are meditating on Christ's life. We cannot pray three rosaries fervently and not stay focused on Christ.

About the Windows

The windows are very important to this plan of the Father. He wants people to go from window to window and pray at each window the mysteries of the rosary.

The Annunciation is across from the Assumption. We see the plan of the Father unfold in the life of Mary from the greeting of the angel Gabriel until she is taken up, body and soul, into heaven.

Do we not see that this is the same plan of the Father unfolding in our life? We struggle, we are joyful, we do ordinary things. We sometimes feel as if we are carrying a cross and falling to the ground. We are persecuted and we feel we are being crowned with thorns, but there is always the resurrection when we experience His life deeper and deeper and we know He lives.

The windows show the lives of Jesus and Mary. As we walk from window to window we watch our spiritual life unfold in Him. Each window and its location are part of the Father's Plan. He wants people to pray the rosary and walk, as Christ walked, and live His life in our life.

The Annunciation is opposite the Assumption and so the Father's plan unfolds in our lives from our conception in our mother's womb to our death when we too, hopefully, will be taken into heaven.

We see the Visitation. Mary goes to share the good news with one person, her cousin Elizabeth.

The window opposite shows the Descent of the Holy Spirit on the Apostles. The Apostles are sent out to share the good news to the world. We are His modern-day apostles, sharing the good news, the message of His love and His life to the world. We too are sent by the Holy Spirit and Mary our Mother is forever with us.

We see Jesus, the little Shepherd, born, surrounded by little sheep. Even as a little child, He is the Chief Shepherd of the Flock.

Across from this window is the Ascension into Heaven. We see Jesus going into heaven and leaving His shepherds behind to carry out His work. He came to show us the way. He came as a baby to give love and He ascends into heaven, leaving us to give His love to others.

We see the Presentation in the Temple. Simeon blessed them and said to Mary, His mother: 'Look, he is destined for the fall and for the rise of many in Israel, destined to be a sign that is opposed—and a sword will pierce your soul too.' (Lk 2:34-35). This window is opposite the Resurrection. Once we encounter Christ we are never the same. We can choose life or death.

The Resurrection window is right next to the Crucifixion. I love these two windows. I see Jesus, battered and bruised, bloodied and dead for love of me and I see Him at the next window, radiant and glistening in glory, victorious. Oh, how I love these two windows! Our whole life, a constant dying and rising in Him.

We see the joy of young Mary as she brings her Son to present Him to the Father. The news of Simeon is a sword in her heart. He tells her of the sufferings to come. We see the death and resurrection in the windows across the Chapel. We see a baby-in-arms. We know the prophesy given; the prophesy is fulfilled. We see the crucified and resurrected Christ in the windows opposite the Presentation.

We see the Child Jesus in the temple. We know of the separation between Jesus and Mary. Across from this window we see the Crucifixion. From the prophecy of Simeon Mary knew of the sufferings to come. She had a constant ache in her heart. Jesus and Mary both shared this secret deep in their hearts. Her heart was so joined to His from the first moment of conception. This separation between Jesus and Mary was a foreshadowing of the separation to come. We see the loss of the Child Jesus in the temple and the window opposite is that separation between Jesus and Mary by His death on the cross. Next to His death is the Resurrection. He was lost for three days in the temple, He was locked in the tomb for three days, but He rose on the third day.

Mary's heart is so closely connected to the Heart of Christ. His Heart was formed in her body through the power of the Holy Spirit. It is through this pierced heart the life in the Church flows. Mary gave Him His life through her body. He gives us His Divine Life through this Heart, formed in her body. Divine Life flows from the Father, in the Holy Spirit, through the pierced Heart of Jesus, through Mary's heart to us.

If we walk these windows we see the close connection between Jesus and Mary. His Heart is within her body for the first two mysteries. Although she is a separate body, when He is born, He receives His food from Mary's breast. In the fourth window, she is still providing Him with His food.

It is through Mary we receive His life.

In the back of the Chapel are the Sorrowful Mysteries. It is through His immense suffering that we realize more fully His overwhelming love for us. In His Divine Knowing, He knew all the anguish and suffering that He would undergo. Because of His great love for us He accepted the Will of the Father and suffered immense torture to His death on the cross. It is a great experience to view all five mysteries together for we see His willingness to suffer for love of us.

In praying the rosary, all through our walk we are seeing the compliance of Jesus and Mary to the Will of the Father. He is bound in a baby body. He is tied at the pillar. He is nailed on a cross. He always complied to the Father's Will.

We see how Mary complies to the Will of the Father. She says "yes" in every window. She says "yes" to the angel. She says "yes" to His birth. He was born in such poverty. She says "yes" to the prophecy of Simeon, carrying the great suffering within her pure heart. She says "yes" when she stands beneath the cross and watches Jesus die. She says "yes" at the Resurrection, at the Ascension, and at the Descent of the Holy Spirit. Her reward is that she is taken into heaven, body and soul, and in the final window, which is separate, she is crowned Queen of Heaven and Earth.

Oh, the beatific vision when we are wrapped with Love itself, we will exist completely in Him, when there is no time, no fear. Oh, the glory that awaits us for serving the Lord, we will be united with God Himself and completely satisfied! In praying the rosary, His life lives in our life. He no longer walks the earth; He lives in us. As we walk, as we talk, as we love, we carry Christ alive within us in this world today. Mary carried the Child Jesus in her womb. We carry His life within us. Oh, that we would walk as He wills us to walk!

The Incarnation goes on. We are constantly being formed within the womb of Mary through the Holy Spirit to be more and more like Christ. This is our spiritual journey to our glory!

The first ten windows show Jesus and Mary as they walked the earth. His divinity is hidden all through His Passion, but the glory shines forth in the Glorious Mysteries. Christ rises from the dead and ascends into heaven. The Holy Spirit comes and sends His apostles out with the good news. Mary is taken into heaven and crowned Queen.

We walk the earth. We do not see the glory. Heaven and hell are realities. I cry when I meditate on the Resurrection. No matter how hard it seems here, I know that He is risen. He is alive and the victory is won.

Mary appeared almost every day for fourteen months at Our Lady of the Holy Spirit Center. God has chosen Our Lady of the Holy Spirit Center as a special place. It is Mary's house. Divinity has contacted man there with these revelations. Many of my experiences, visions and messages were received there. God's Blue Books and Rosaries from the Hearts of Jesus and Mary are important messages from God to help bring about the reign of the Sacred Heart and the triumph of the Immaculate Heart of Mary. Jesus and Mary wish all to pray and walk the rosary in the Rosary Chapel.

Jesus is using the Shepherds of Christ Movement in a powerful way to renew the Church and the world. This chosen instrument of Our Lord will greatly bring about the completion of the Fatima message. He has called His special apostles in the Shepherds of Christ Movement, under the direction of Fr. Edward Carter, S.J., spiritual director and founder of the Shepherds of Christ Movement, to go into the churches, schools and families to spread the consecration to the Hearts of Jesus and Mary.

Available are all of the materials that He has given to help bring about this renewal. By contacting Shepherds of Christ Ministries, you can receive information that will help you to carry out their request. Jesus is encouraging His special apostles to contact priests and ask them if they are receiving the priestly newsletter *Shepherds of Christ.* He is asking His apostles to set up prayer chapters, centered in consecration, in churches, schools, meeting places and homes. It is in consecration that we will comply with Our Lady's request made at Fatima.

May the Sacred Heart of Jesus reign and the Immaculate Heart of Mary triumph!

Mary said until a sufficient number have consecrated their hearts to the Hearts of Jesus and Mary, we will not have peace in the world. She now appears to me as *Our Lady of the Holy Rosary.* She appeared first as *Our Lady of Light,* then as *Our Lady of Sorrows,* and lastly, as *Our Lady of the Holy Rosary.* It is through Shepherds of Christ Ministries that we are complying to Our Lady's request and spreading the Consecration to the Two Hearts and the Rosary to the world. On the feast of the Sorrowful Mother, September 15, 1995, Mary told me that I would continue to suffer until I spread the Rosary to the world.

From these teachings, I love the Rosary with all my heart. I hope that these meditations and messages from the Hearts of Jesus and Mary will lead you to the deepest union with Their Hearts. I love you and ask you to follow Our Lady's request and pray the Rosary and to help spread the Rosary to the world. Our Lady told St. Dominic that the Rosary and the Scapular will be great instruments in the salvation of the world. Please write to Shepherds of Christ Ministries and help Jesus and Mary, for the time is urgent.

The Chapel and the Windows

As envisioned for the original complex called Mount St. Mary of the West Seminary, the Rosary Chapel occupied the geographical center of a large educational/residential/worship facility befitting a major seminary. If one were to draw the chapel, then ring it with a maize of corridors, walkways, courtyards, business offices, classrooms and, yes, even practice altars, one would get an impression

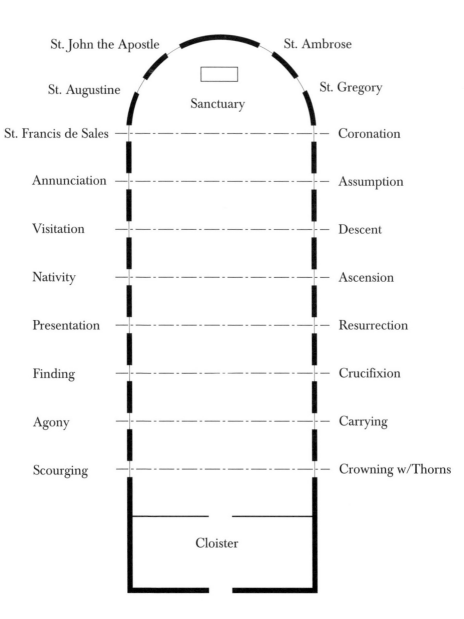

St. John the Apostle — St. Ambrose

St. Augustine — St. Gregory

Sanctuary

St. Francis de Sales — Coronation

Annunciation — Assumption

Visitation — Descent

Nativity — Ascension

Presentation — Resurrection

Finding — Crucifixion

Agony — Carrying

Scourging — Crowning w/Thorns

Cloister

ROSARY CHAPEL WINDOWS
Our Lady of the Holy Spirit Center
Norwood, Ohio

of the important, central role the chapel played in the life of the residents. The front and wings of the complex housed auditorium, cafeteria, classrooms, student dormitories and faculty offices, giving the main edifice an imposing three-story height above ground. Still, the chapel was so central in fact that, if one walked straight on a straight line through the main entry door, one would enter the main chapel in a direct line toward the main altar.

Originally designed with classic facing side choir stalls common in monasteries and large basilicas, the main chapel was meant to set a tone of profound dignity for the aspiring clerics who worshiped there. As shown in the accompanying sketch, entry to the chapel was by way of a small cloister where visitors could participate in certain ceremonies being celebrated in the chapel beyond. The choir loft immediately above the cloister housed the chapel organ and space for the attendant choir when the occasion dictated.

Walls and ceiling were decorated in a subtle mixture of arches and fluted columns–true beauty through simplicity–but what set the spiritual tone of the chapel were its stained glass windows. The windows above the sanctuary featured five Doctors of the Church (Saints Francis de Sales, Augustine, Jerome, Ambrose and Gregory), all positive role models for aspiring young seminarians. Then, starting on the front left as one faces the altar, and continuing clockwise, came the 15 windows dedicated to the 15 decades of the rosary. It is important to note the orientation of the windows since, on several occasions in this book, a feature of a mystery depicted in, say, a Joyful Mystery window on the left wall is compared with a corresponding feature in a Glorious Mystery window on the wall opposite.

Thus, just as the rosary truths depicted in the windows were critical to the formation of priests 75 years ago, so they continue today to influence the spiritual well-being of all who visit this chapel.

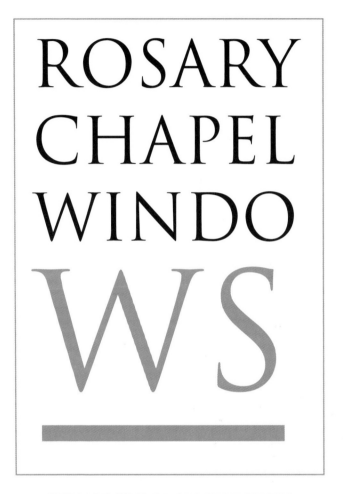

ROSARY CHAPEL WINDOWS

OUR LADY OF THE HOLY SPIRIT CENTER
NORWOOD, OHIO

The Annunciation
THE FIRST JOYFUL MYSTERY

The Visitation
THE SECOND JOYFUL MYSTERY

The Birth of Our Lord
THE THIRD JOYFUL MYSTERY

The Presentation of Our Lord in the Temple
THE FOURTH JOYFUL MYSTERY

The Finding of Our Lord in the Temple
THE FIFTH JOYFUL MYSTERY

The Agony in the Garden
THE FIRST SORROWFUL MYSTERY

The Scourging at the Pillar
THE SECOND SORROWFUL MYSTERY

The Crowning with Thorns
THE THIRD SORROWFUL MYSTERY

Jesus Carries His Cross
THE FOURTH SORROWFUL MYSTERY

Jesus Dies on the Cross
THE FIFTH SORROWFUL MYSTERY

The Resurrection
THE FIRST GLORIOUS MYSTERY

The Ascension
THE SECOND GLORIOUS MYSTERY

The Descent of the Holy Spirit
THE THIRD GLORIOUS MYSTERY

The Assumption of Our Lady into Heaven
THE FOURTH GLORIOUS MYSTERY

The Coronation of Our Lady
THE FIFTH GLORIOUS MYSTERY

44

1. **The Prophecy of Simeon.**
Simeon tells Mary that a
sword will pierce her heart.

2. **The Flight into Egypt.**
Mary and Joseph flee with
Jesus to safety from Herod.

3. **The Loss of the
Child Jesus.**
Mary and Joseph
desperately seek
their son in
Jerusalem.

4. **Mary Meets Jesus on the
Way to Calvary.**
Mother and Son share the
agony of the cross.

THE SEVEN SORROWS OF THE BLESSED VIRGIN MARY

7. **The Burial of Jesus.**
Mary suffers the final agony
of her Son's entombment.

6. **Mary Holds Jesus.**
One last time
mother cradles her
Son in her arms.

5. **Jesus Dies on the Cross**
Mary watches as Jesus gives
His last for mankind.

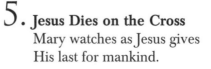

The Rosary

by Rita Ring

ROSARY MEDITATIONS

CHRISTMAS DAY CHILDREN'S ROSARY
DECEMBER 25, 1994
THE JOYFUL MYSTERIES

The Annunciation
1. The Angel Gabriel appeared to Mary and asked Mary to be the Mother of Jesus.
2. Mary always complied with the Will of the Father. She said "yes" to the angel.
3. She was filled with the Holy Spirit and the Word was made flesh.
4. *Song:* Come Holy Ghost…
5. There was such intimacy between Mary and Jesus from the first moment of conception.
6. She felt the life of the child Jesus grow within her womb.
7. It was in her womb that the Most Sacred Heart of Jesus was formed through the Holy Spirit.
8. It is in realizing this connection between the Hearts of Jesus and Mary that we will grow in greater union with God.
9. The Holy Spirit forever transforms us more and more into the image of Jesus.
10. The womb of the Virgin Mary is the holy dwelling place of our beloved Savior.

The Visitation
1. Mary, being pregnant herself, but hearing through the angel that Elizabeth had conceived a child in her old age, made haste to the hill country to be with her cousin Elizabeth.
2. When she arrived, the child in Elizabeth's womb leapt for joy.
3. Mary was filled with the Holy Spirit and cried out in a loud voice the Magnificat.
4. Mary said, "My soul proclaims the greatness of the Lord and

47

my spirit rejoices in God my Savior." (Lk 1:46,47)

5. "...because he has looked upon the humiliation of his servant. Yes, from now onwards all generations will call me blessed." (Lk 1:48)

6. "...for the Almighty has done great things for me. Holy is his name." (Lk 1:49)

7. Jesus is no less present this day in the Eucharist than He was in Mary's womb.

8. How He waits and yearns for us to come and to be with Him because He loves us so much!

9. If we realized how much He loves us, we would never fear.

10. *Song:* O come, O come, Emmanuel, and ransom captive Israel, that mourns in lonely exile here, until the Son of God appears. Rejoice! Rejoice! Emmanuel shall come to you, O Israel!

Birth of Jesus

1. Think of the glorious night when Jesus was born in a stable. The angels sang and shepherds watched.

2. The cows and the sheep were there to keep them warm.

3. This is truly Jesus Christ, the Son of God, who humbled Himself to share in our humanity.

4. *Song:* Angels we have heard on high, sweetly singing o'er the plains. And the mountains in reply, echoing their joyous strains.

5. *Song:* Gloria in excelsis Deo, Gloria in excelsis Deo.

6. *Song:* Away in a manger, no crib for a bed, the little Lord Jesus lay down His sweet head. The stars in the sky looked down where He lay, the little Lord Jesus asleep on the hay.

7. *Song:* O come let us adore Him, O come let us adore Him, O come let us adore Him, Christ the Lord.

8. *Song:* What child is this who lay to rest, on Mary's lap is sleeping? Whom angels greet with anthem sweet, while shepherds watch are keeping.

9. See Jesus, Mary and Joseph in the stable and see the tenderness in the eyes of Mary as she gazes on her newborn baby child, who is truly God!

10. The birth of Jesus is at the heart of salvation history.

The Presentation of Jesus in the Temple

1. Mary and Joseph took the child Jesus to the temple.

2. While they were there, the prophet Simeon prophesied the sufferings of Jesus and Mary to come.

3. Simeon said to Mary, "…and a sword will pierce your soul, too." (Lk 2:35)
4. As he prophesied the sufferings of Jesus and Mary, he also prophesied how many souls would be saved through Jesus.
5. Mary gazes so tenderly on her precious child and, from this moment on, every time she looked at Jesus, she remembered the prophecy of Simeon.
6. She had a constant ache in her Heart since the prophecy of Simeon.
7. *Song:* See the eyes that look at Mary, her tender infant Child…
8. She looked at the baby Jesus. She held Him in her arms. All through their life together, she knew His Heart. There was such love from the moment of conception between her and her Son! There was such intimacy between the Heart of Jesus and the Heart of Mary.
9. Dear Mary, you knew the Heart of your beloved Son Jesus. Please lead us to closer intimacy with Him. It is in loving Him through your pure and tender Heart that I too will love Him more tenderly.
10. Let us love, through your Heart, our beloved Father, Son and Holy Spirit.

The Finding of the Child Jesus in the Temple

1. How the Heart of Mary knew the Heart of Jesus! How the Heart of Mary suffered every sorrow. How she suffered when they lost the child Jesus in the temple.
2. She calls out to us today to pray for her little lost children of the world.
3. "It happened that, three days later, they found him in the Temple, sitting among the teachers, listening to them, and asking them questions; and all those who heard him were astounded at his intelligence and his replies." (Lk 2:46,47)
4. When His parents saw Him "…his mother said to him, 'My child, why have you done this to us? See how worried your father and I have been, looking for you?" (Lk 2:48)
5. "He went down with them then and came to Nazareth and lived under their authority. His mother stored up all these things in her heart." (Luke 2:51)
6. She was His Mother. She took care of Him. She knew Him with a deep, motherly love in her Heart.

7. **Mary:** My beloved children, pray to the child Jesus. He will answer your prayers.

8. I see Mary before me alive many times when I pray this mystery of the rosary. I see her and hear her call out. She begs us to pray for her lost children so that they will not be condemned to hell for their sinfulness and willfulness.

9. **Mary:** I am Mary, your mother. I am urgently calling you to spread the love of My Son Jesus to the world. Make this your Christmas gift to this world: to help spread these rosaries from the Hearts of Jesus and Mary. Please spread them to the children and the adults.

10. *Song:* O come, little children…

March 18, 1995

Jesus: These are My messages for My beloved ones. I am handling this. You are unaware of what is coming. You must pray constantly for all you work with. Satan wants you stopped, and the rosary stopped, now!

I am giving all involved this letter, asking them to pray and read My letters. It is in focusing on Me, My love, that you will fight off Satan's attacks. I ask one hour daily in adoration before the tabernacle.

The rosary is given as a gift from Our Hearts to this world. Do not underestimate the power of the rosary. Prayed this way, I will give you many graces, graces that will open hearts to the messages. This rosary is given to the world. This is a special gift from Our Hearts.

I want this book to be entitled, *Rosaries from the Hearts of Jesus and Mary,* received and given daily at Our Lady of the Holy Spirit Center, Norwood, Ohio to Rita Ring, Marty Coby and the Ring children, Cathy and Joseph Ring. Messages are transcribed from tapes by Marty Coby. Other rosaries from other locations may be included. Father Edward Carter, S.J., spiritual consultant for these rosary meditations and messages.

April 9, 1995

Jesus: I want My beloved priests to pray the rosary and use these meditations. The people's hearts will be brought back to My Heart and My Mother's Heart. These are rosaries from the Hearts of Jesus and Mary. They are a powerful tool to spread the devotion to the rosary across this land. People can lead the rosary in prayer groups. Make the shorter meditations into large print for nursing homes. Make some meditations into large print for the sick who have all day to pray. It is only through the power of prayer that Satan will be stopped. Praying the rosary will crush the head of Satan. You are given these rosary meditations as a powerful tool to crush the head of Satan and bring the hearts of all to the Hearts of Jesus and Mary. They are focused on the Eucharist and the Mass and will lead many to the Catholic Church.

I am giving all who promote the spread of these messages great graces and guiding them as they do. Teams can be started to go out and pray the rosary this way. Make recordings for the blind and the old.

I am Jesus. Please comply with My request.

ROSARY MEDITATIONS
JANUARY 26, 1995
THE SORROWFUL MYSTERIES

The Agony in the Garden

1. **R.** Be with Jesus as He kneels in the Garden of Gethsemane.
2. **R.** Be there in the night. Hear the sounds of the night. See Jesus as He kneels in such agony to see before Him all the sufferings that He is about to undergo.
3. **R.** With greatest love for each one of us, the Father sent into this world His only-begotten Son.
4. **R.** Jesus took on a human nature with greatest love for each one of us. He now kneels in the Garden, His Heart in such anguish. He who is Love sees before Him all the souls from all time who would neglect Him and treat Him so indifferently despite all His suffering and love that His most tender Heart has for each and every soul.
5. **R.** He saw before Him all the souls that would be condemned to eternal damnation despite the fact that He suffered and died for love of each soul.
6. **R.** The anguish that He suffered in the Garden, the agonies that

He suffered in His most Sacred Heart, were far greater than the physical wounds that He would soon bear throughout His entire Passion. For He is Love, with a Heart burning for love of all souls–the souls that neglect Him, the souls that do not even think of Him, the souls that go through their lives, have nothing to do with Jesus, and then are condemned forever and ever to the fires of hell.

7. **R.** Jesus remains with us this very day, the same as the day that He knelt in the Garden. He remains with us in His divinity and humanity. With greatest love for each one of us He longs, He thirsts, He waits for us to come and be with Him in front of the tabernacle.

8. His suffering in the Garden was so great that His sweat became as great drops of blood upon the ground.

9. **R.** He went to the apostles and asked them, "Had you not the strength to stay awake one hour?" (Mk 14:37) How many times does Jesus ask us this day if we do not have one hour to spend with Him? There are twenty-four hours in a day. But how many times during the day do we say no to Jesus, that we are too busy. And His Heart waits and waits for us. At every second His Heart is an endless, burning furnace of love. Whether we think of Him or not, He is always ablaze, on fire for us, loving us and waiting for us to allow Him to be our constant companion.

10. **R.** God, grant to us the grace to know and to love You more so that we can more fully realize that You truly are God-made-man in Jesus Christ, that You come to this earth in greatest love for each one of us, that You long and wait for our love and that You want to give us Your love.

Song between decades: I come to you with greatest love, I am your loving Savior. I am your God, I died for you. I come to you this day.

The Scourging at the Pillar

1. **Jesus:** My Heart is on fire for each one of My precious souls. I long for you to come and be with Me. As I suffered all through My Passion, the greatest agonies were not the agonies that I suffered to My body–the scourging at the pillar, the tearing of My flesh–but the agonies that I endured to My most tender Heart, which is a Heart of love waiting to share with each and every one of My precious souls. Oh, My children, I call out to you this

day to spread My love to the world that is in pain. I call out to you to be My soldiers, to spread the love of My Most Sacred Heart to the souls that are suffering and in pain. You are My mighty warriors in a world that is cold and has forgotten God. You must be strong soldiers, for this world will persecute you as they persecuted Me. I send you into the world, armed with hearts filled with My love, to spread My love along the high-ways and the byways in every corner of this earth and I ask you this day, can you say no?

2. **Jesus:** They tied Me to a pillar and they beat My flesh. My once unblemished back was now an open wound. I was full of blood. But My worst agony was the agony that I endured in My Most Sacred Heart, the Heart that gives to you and to every soul divine love, divine life, and is rejected by many, is treated coldly.

3. **Jesus:** I loved Judas so dearly and Judas betrayed Me with a kiss. How many of My dear souls come to Me with hearts that are hot and cold. I want you to come to Me with hearts, full of love, that will unite with Mine, that will become one with Mine, that will give to this world My love for your hurting brothers. I ask you this day, "Do not say no!" I am truly Jesus Christ, the Son of God, Who was scourged at the pillar for love of your brothers. I ask you to hear the blows that they gave to Me. They are the blows that I suffered for your brother. How can you treat your brother badly when they tore My flesh, and out of greatest love I withstood all this treatment for your beloved brother?

4. **Jesus:** I gave My all. I stood there. I was beaten. I was bruised. I was bloodied. I came to show you the way, the way to love. They persecuted Me. I loved those who persecuted Me. I ask you this day to be kind in your heart, to give to this world the love that I want to give to you. I am a burning furnace of endless love. My power never goes out. My love is never spent. Come to My Most Sacred Heart and I will fill your hearts with endless love.

5. *Song:* Lord, let me walk that last mile in Your shoes, under the weight of the wood…

6. **Jesus:** See in the dim light as I stand at the pillar. See the men with their angry faces, with hatred in their hearts, as they pound at My flesh.

7. **Jesus:** When they persecute you and hate you because you are

not of this world, you must endure all out of greatest love. My way is always love. I came to show you the way, the way to eternal happiness. It is only in loving one another that you will merit eternal life. I ask you for two things. I ask you to love God and to love one another.

8. **Jesus:** Come to My Eucharistic Heart! Let Me fill you with the fire of My love so that it will radiate to all those that you come in contact with. For the power of the Almighty God is a power that cannot be contained. It will radiate from your being to all those you touch.

9. **Jesus:** When I walked from the pillar, the earth was marked by My bloody footprints.

10. **Jesus:** As the earth was marked by My bloody footprints, I ask you to make a mark on this world, to spread to this world the love of My Most Sacred Heart.

Song between decades: I come to you with greatest love…

The Crowning with Thorns

1. **Jesus:** My body was battered, bruised and bloodied, and they covered Me with a dirty purple robe that they put on top of My wounds. I held a scepter and they crowned Me with a sharp crown of piercing thorns.

2. **R.** Do you know what it is like to get a little splinter in your hand? They pounded into Jesus' most precious head thorns that were thick and piercing until the blood ran down His face, into His eyes and into His ears. His hair was matted. This was truly the King of Kings! The Son of God! And He was crowned with a crown of piercing thorns!

3. *Song:* Only this I want, but to know the Lord, and to bear His cross, so to wear the crown He wore…

4. **Jesus:** They spit on Me and they hollered slanders at Me and I sat, as they did, in silence.

5. **Jesus:** I truly came into this world, the Son of God, to show you the way. As I sat in silence, think of how you respond to those who come to you with hatred in their hearts. My way is the way of love. You must love all your brothers as I have loved.

6. **Jesus:** My Father created each and every child—so precious, so unique—with such love that He sent Me into this world.

7. **Jesus:** I love you so this day that I would suffer again all that I suffered for you before.

8. **Jesus:** With all the love that I pour out to each and every one of you, think of how it is to love so much and to be neglected by so many.

9. **Jesus:** Pray to the Spirit to open your heart to the fire of My love.

10. **Jesus:** You are blind men! You do not see the love that I outpour to you. You see little incidental things, so close in front of your face, when My Heart is overflowing with divine love, with divine life. I want to give you My life! I give you Myself in the Eucharist. Come for My love. Nothing on this earth can compare to My divine love and My divine life that I want to give to you!

Song between decades: I come to you with greatest love...

The Carrying of the Cross

1. **R.** See Jesus with His hands tied, with a look of perfect peace on His face. And see those men who are surrounding Jesus, with their sharp instruments poking at Him with anger and hatred on their faces—such anger and hatred that they condemned Jesus to death on a cross!

2. **R.** They gave to Him a heavy cross that they put on His most precious shoulder. He carried the weight of the sins of the world on His back. This is the love that He has for each and every man, that He carries the cross with our sins on His back.

3. **R.** He calls out to us that He is no less present in the Eucharist this day than the day He walked to Calvary with His cross on His back. And He says to each one of us, "I give you Myself. Why do you run from My altar when I, Jesus Christ, the Son of God, come to you and become one with you, and you run from the Church?"

4. **Jesus:** I peered into the eyes of My beloved mother and she peered into My eyes. There was joy at the meeting of the eyes, but such sorrow deep within each of Our Hearts. The knowing of My mother, the knowing of Me, her most precious Son, and how she had held Me and loved Me! I saw her in such suffering! I saw her face with tears. I saw My most precious mother torn so deeply in her Heart. It is the love of Our Hearts for you that has led us to this place. I ask you to spread this love throughout the world. I would truly carry My cross this day for you because I love you so dearly. My children! My children! What more do you want than that God comes to earth and is born a man out of

greatest love for you? And you in your limited vision see only in front of your face. You do not come to My altar to receive the life that I want to outpour to you. My children! My children! You are so blind! Pray for grace! Pray for My life, to know and love all that you do not see. You do not see because you do not come to My altar, because you do not spend time with Me!

5. **Jesus:** My mother comes to stay, to lead you ever closer to My most tender Heart. I ask you to answer this call, the call of the Immaculate Heart of Mary and the Sacred Heart of Jesus, to be joined ever closer to the Hearts brimming over with love for each and every soul.

6. **Jesus:** I fell under My cross. The weight was so heavy! I did not give My cross up. I willingly carried this cross for love of you!

7. **Jesus:** It is in living in the Father's Will that you will be the happiest. To My very death I followed the Will of the Father.

8. *Song:* See the eyes that look at Mary, her tender infant child. See the child's Heart beat so tenderly, the Savior of the world.

9. **R.** See through the eyes of Mary. She peered into Jesus' eyes on Calvary. See through the eyes of Mary as she comes and appears to us this day to tell us to see her through her eyes the love of her precious Son, Jesus Christ, to see that He truly walked to Calvary, that He was truly scourged and crowned with thorns and that He did it for greatest love of each of us. And He calls out this day for us to come and be with Him and to spread His love to this world.

10. *Song:* She rocked Him as a baby. She fed Him as a child. She heard Him call Her name out in the night. She helped Him take His first step and she cried when He said His first words. I wish they all could see through a Mother's eyes.

Song between decades: I come to you with greatest love…

The Crucifixion and Death of Jesus on the Cross

1. **R.** See the little hands of Jesus. See the little feet of Jesus as Mary holds Him as a baby. And now she stands and watches as they pound nails through His most precious hands into the cross. The anguish in her Heart so deep! And a sword, too, shall pierce your Heart, Oh Mary!

2. **R.** Mary does not bear the wounds, the blood, as Jesus does. But Mary's Heart is torn to see her beloved Son, battered, bruised and bloody, and now hanging on the cross!

3. **R.** Be there! The sky has turned dark as Jesus hangs for three agonizing hours on the cross. His body is humped over. He is so weak! He gives His blood. He spreads His arms. He gives His all for love of each and every one of us. He truly gives His flesh. He gives His blood because He loves us so much! He was born a human! He was born on bare wood in a stable and now He hangs on a cross!

4. **R.** His blood was spent so that we could inherit eternal life.

5. **R.** As He gave His life on the cross, so He gives us His life this day in the Eucharist!

6. *Song:* I am the Bread of Life. He who comes to Me shall not hunger and who believes in Me shall not thirst. No one can come to Me unless the Father beckons. And I will raise you up, and I will raise you up, and I will raise you up on the last day.

7. **R.** He gave the last beat of His Heart. He gave His last breath. He gave His all. His hands were punctured with nails. His Head was pierced with thorns. He gave the inside of His body as well as the outside of His body! And He asks us, in greatest love, to surrender ourselves to Him. For He truly gave His all for love of us. If He loved us so much that He gave His body, His blood, His all for each and every one of us, would He not give us from His abundance this day? He comes with such letters of love to tell you that He is truly Jesus Christ, the Son of God, and in your midst this day in the Eucharist, waiting for you to come and be with Him, for He truly loves with a Heart of divine love. He truly has divine life that He outpours to each and every soul. He wants so much to share Himself with each one of us!
Jesus: "Come to Me, My children, and I will give you My divine love, My divine life. I love you so dearly! I call out to you this day to come for My love and to give this love to the world for it is only through you that the Father's plan will be realized. For a heart fixed on the love of God can move a mountain. I am asking you to live in the Father's Will, to spread My love throughout the world. If you say no, this world will suffer. You are My chosen ones, each and every soul. Come! Be filled with the love I pour out to you. Love your fellowmen. Love your brothers when they hate you and persecute you. Love them as I loved those who put Me to death. I ask you this day to open your hearts and rid yourselves of all impurities, to

pray to the Spirit to sanctify your hearts, to clean out the debris of hatred and anger, and to come to My tabernacle with a heart that is open and pure so I can fill you with My divine love. For it is in your uniting with Me that I can operate from you and love this world as I so desire. This is My call to you this day. Can you say no? See Me hanging on the cross. This is how I loved you!

8. **R.** Mary stood under the cross and she saw Her beloved Son as He took His last breath.
9. **R.** She calls out to you this day. She is calling! She is calling each and every soul that He gave His life for to know His love. For it is only in this love that you will find what your soul craves.
10. **R.** And they gave to Mary the lifeless body of her precious Son. As she held His baby body tenderly in her arms, she—so weak!— now holds His lifeless body in her arms, covered with blood.

ROSARY MEDITATIONS
FEBRUARY 1, 1995
THE JOYFUL MYSTERIES

The Annunciation
1. The Angel Gabriel appeared to Mary and asked her to be the mother of Jesus.
2. Mary always complied with the Will of the Father. She said, "...let it happen to me as you have said." (Lk 1:38)
3. Mary was filled with the Holy Spirit, and the Word became flesh.
4. There was always great intimacy between Jesus and His mother. From the first moment of conception she felt the life of Jesus, Son of God, grow within her womb.
5. The child Jesus is with us this day. He is in our brothers. He is in our children. If the child Jesus were here and we were to hold Him, to talk to and be with Him, we would treat Him with such joy and such kindness! Jesus is in our brothers. Jesus is in our children. Jesus is here this day. Do we treat our brothers, our children, one another, with the same kindness that we would the child Jesus?

6. The invisible Jesus was inside of Mary's womb. He was there in His divinity and His humanity. He was God from the first moment of conception. The invisible Jesus remains with us today in the tabernacle. He is present there in His divinity and humanity. We do not see Him, but He is no less present in the tabernacle than the day Mary carried Him in her womb.

7. God is Love! He calls out to us to come to Him, to be close to Him. He truly waits for us in the tabernacle. He is a prisoner awaiting those He loves, the precious souls. So many forget Him day after day while He, the Son of God, waits and waits to share His love with the precious souls that He came to this earth to save.

8. He calls out to us, "Do you not have one hour to watch with Me, the Son of God? I, God, Who came to this earth and was born a human for love of you! I call out to you this day. Take Me seriously! I am truly here, no less present than on the day that Mary carried Me in her womb, and I wait for you with a Heart that is overflowing with divine love and divine life. Can you say no to this divine love that I want to outpour to you?"

9. It was in the womb of the Blessed Virgin Mary that the Most Sacred Heart of Jesus was formed. Jesus took on our human nature out of great love for us.

10. Jesus was carried in Mary's womb. Her womb was a temple to hold the precious Child. She is the Mother of God!

Song between decades: Ave, ave, ave, Maria. Ave, ave, ave, Maria.

The Visitation

1. The angel had told Mary that her cousin Elizabeth had conceived a child. Mary made haste to the hill country to visit her.

2. Upon Mary's arrival at Elizabeth's house, Elizabeth was filled with the Holy Spirit and cried out with a loud voice, "Of all women you are the most blessed, and blessed is the fruit of your womb." (Lk 1:42)

3. "Why should I be honoured with a visit from the mother of my Lord?" (Lk 1:43) Usually the servant goes to the master. But Mary, with the Almighty God within her womb, went to visit Elizabeth.

4. Jesus waits for us this day. He is God and He waits in the tabernacle for us to come and be with Him. He comes to us in the Eucharist. He is the Almighty God and He waits for mere

humans to come and share His love.

5. We receive so much love from God! The Father loved us so much that He sent His only begotten Son into this world so that we might be saved. Jesus waits this very day for us to come and be with Him. It is out of great love that the Master waits for us.

6. When Mary and Jesus arrived at Elizabeth's house, the child in Elizabeth's womb leapt for joy. John, who was to announce the good news that Jesus had come to this earth, even before his birth leapt with joy in the womb of his mother at the presence of Jesus in Mary's womb.

7. Should we not leap for joy? Jesus Christ, the Son of God, born of the Virgin Mary, waits for us this day, no less present than the day He was carried in Mary's womb to the home of her cousin Elizabeth. We take His presence so lightly! We do not see, so we do not realize that God, in His humanity and divinity, is truly present in the tabernacle and waiting for us this very day.

8. Mary was filled with the Holy Spirit and cried out, with a loud voice, her Magnificat: "My soul proclaims the greatness of the Lord and my spirit rejoices in God my Saviour!" (Lk 1:46,47)

9. "…because he has looked on the humiliation of his servant. Yes, from now onwards all generations will call me blessed." (Lk 1:48)

10. "…for the Almighty has done great things for me. Holy is his name."

Song between decades: Ave, ave, ave Maria....

The Birth of Jesus

1. The Father bridges the gap between divinity and humanity in the person of Jesus Christ.

2. Jesus came into this world. Jesus Christ, the only begotten Son of the Father, equal in every way to the Father, came into this world as a little baby, a helpless little baby. If we realized the true majesty of God, if we saw Him in all His majesty, we could not even stand to look at Him. But Jesus, clothed in flesh, comes as a helpless little baby, born in a little crib in a stable in Bethlehem!

3. Do we realize the immense love that the Father has for us that He sent His only begotten Son into this world as a human in the person of Jesus Christ?

4. Jesus, a divine Person, unites His human nature and His divine nature in His Person.

5. Who are we that God loves us so much that He would take on a human nature!

6. We become brothers of God!

7. He comes, the Son of God, in such quiet and such poverty! There is not a roll of drums or a blare of trumpets. He comes in such quiet and a star shines on Him. Is this not how it is when we receive Him in the Eucharist? We ascend the altar. There is not a roll of drums. There is not a blare of trumpets. Quietly we approach the altar and we truly receive God! He comes to us and enters our body in such love! Who are we that God remains with us this day in such love and comes to us to be so closely united to us!?

8. We see the consecrated Host. But within the consecrated Host is truly God, in His divinity and His humanity.

9. We look for those things that are visible. But are not the true treasures found in those things that are invisible? The reality is that this is God's world! We see the things in front of our face and we do not realize how the world of Jesus and Mary truly is. We do not realize how they are with us this very day. Jesus Christ, the Son of God, remains with us this day in His divinity and humanity in the Eucharist. We are surrounded by His presence in one another. He dwells and lives in each one of us when we are in the state of grace. In every blade of grass, the life that is there comes from God. Yet we are so blind! We see so little! Holy Spirit, open up our eyes. Where we are blind, let us see. Let us see more and more the invisible world. Let us know more and more the presence of God as it is all around us. Help us to see Jesus in each other. Help us to be more aware of Jesus Christ, who is truly present with us in the tabernacle.

10. Open our eyes to see beyond what is visible, Lord. Holy Spirit, help us to see beyond the consecrated Host and see Jesus Christ, the Son of God.

Song between decades: Ave, ave, ave, Maria...

The Presentation of Jesus in the Temple

1. The Holy Spirit told Simeon that he would not die until He saw the child of God. The Holy Spirit led Him into the Temple. Jesus, Mary and Joseph came to the Temple and the old man

was overjoyed at the sight of the child Jesus. He held Him with such joy in his arms and said that now he was ready to die for he had seen God.

2. Holy Spirit, enkindle in us the fire of Your love so we may see more clearly Jesus Christ, Who is with us this very day. So that we may see that He is God and, out of great love for each one of us, remains with us, waits for us, longs for us, and wants us to open our hearts wide so that He may enter in. Remove the blinders from our eyes, dear Holy Spirit, and lead us ever closer to intimacy with Jesus Christ, our beloved Savior.

3. *Song:* Come Holy Ghost, Creator blest, and in our hearts take up Thy rest. Come with Thy grace and heavenly aid to fill the hearts which Thou hast made, to fill the hearts which Thou hast made.

4. Simeon told Joseph and Mary of the great sufferings that Mary and Jesus would have to undergo and he said to Mary, "…and a sword will pierce your soul too." (Lk 2:35)

5. Think of how it would be for Mary to look at her small child Jesus and know that He would experience great suffering. From this point on a sword pierced Mary's Heart. Each time that she beheld her child she remembered the prophecy of Simeon and she suffered.

6. And how Mary suffered! The swords that pierced her Heart so many times through Jesus' life! The sword that pierced her Heart on the way to Calvary as she peered into the eyes of her beloved Son, that gaze that shows to us the great intimacy between the Son and His mother, that Heart that knew her Son so well!

7. Her Heart was pierced with a sword as she stood beneath His cross and watched Him suffer in such anguish for three agonizing hours. The precious Child that she had held in her arms in the Temple when Simeon told her, "…and a sword will pierce your soul too." (Lk 2:35)

8. *Song:* I rocked Him as a baby, I fed Him as a child. I heard Him call my name out in the night. I helped Him take His first step, and I cried when I heard His first words. I wish they all could see through a mother's eyes.

9. Mary, just as you presented the child Jesus in your arms in the temple, tuck us into the Heart of Jesus and present us to our

loving Father so that we may be ever closer and closer to the Heart of Jesus and the Father. And lead us closer to your beloved Spouse, the Holy Spirit.

10. Holy Spirit, the more we unite with Mary, our mother, transform us more and more into the image of Jesus and lead us ever closer to the Father.

Song between decades: Ave, ave, ave, Maria…

The Finding of Jesus in the Temple

1. When Jesus was twelve years old, He was taken up to the Temple for the feast of Passover.
2. When it was over, Mary and Joseph left Jerusalem but the child Jesus remained there.
3. They had gone a day's journey before they realized that the child Jesus had been left behind.
4. With great sorrow in their hearts they returned and searched for the child Jesus.
5. They found Him in the temple where He was teaching the doctors.
6. Jesus, as you taught the doctors in the temple, teach us Your divine truths. Holy Spirit, open our hearts so that we may more and more receive Your gifts to know, love and understand God so that we might grow in greater love and knowledge of our beloved God!
7. And the Holy Spirit came upon them and filled their hearts full of wisdom and knowledge and joy to know more and more the divine truths that the Savior came to give us. His ever burning Heart remains with us this day, this Heart that wants to give to us such love, such life! He imparts this life to us abundantly in the Eucharist whereby He feeds our life. When we come to the Eucharist, He outpours this life, this life of grace. He wants to give us His very life, His Body, His Blood, to nurture and feed our life, and we balk! We stumble. We wander around and complain! And this good God, Who came to this earth and was born a human, gave His flesh and blood and died for us and rose on the third day to give us His life, remains with us this day with His very own flesh and blood to feed this life! He gives us His Word to feed us and we take it so lightly! He calls out ever so gently in His tender voice and with His burning Heart. He calls out to us and says, "Come to me, all you who labor and are

burdened, and I will give you rest!" But in our blindness we turn away and we do not realize the true treasure that is here! This is the Son of God Who remains with us this day, truly present, the same as the day He was in the Temple, the same as the day He hung on the cross, the same as the day He rose from the tomb and ascended into heaven! And He calls out in a gentle voice, with a burning Heart, "My dear children, I long for your love. Open up your hearts to Me. I am the Son of God! I have all the power! You cannot in your foolish ways do anything without Me!"

8. *Song:* I come to you with greatest love. I am your loving Savior. I am your God, I died for you. I come to you this day.

9. Dear Mary, if we ever lose our way from the Most Sacred Heart of your Son, lead us back quickly.
Song: O burning Heart, O Love divine. How sweet You are to me. I see the Host, I know You are here to love and care for me.

10. *Song:* Give me Your Heart, O Jesus. Give me a heart like Yours. Teach me to love You with this new heart. Oh, I know little of how to love You. Create in me, O precious Savior, this loving heart!

STATIONS OF THE CROSS
AT A SHEPHERDS OF CHRIST MEETING
FEBRUARY 22, 1995

1. Jesus Is Condemned to Death

Jesus: My dear child, with angry hearts and hatred on their faces, they poked at Me and condemned Me to death. I stood so silent, My hands tied, in perfect peace, because I knew the Father's love. I knew the Father's Will. You too will stand your trials in perfect peace, the more you realize the immense love the Father, Son and Holy Spirit have for you. Pray to the Spirit to transform you more and more into My image and, through this transformation, you will be led ever closer to the Father. Oh, how I love you!

2. They Give Jesus the Cross

Jesus: They gave Me a heavy cross, laden with the sins of the world. They placed it on My shoulder. It was so heavy I felt as if My shoulder would break. I ask you to carry little crosses, to experience little pains. I could not remove this cross from My shoulder. The weight was unbearable. It is through My suffering and death that you receive new life. It is through your sufferings this day that you will grow in your life with Me. Oh, child, I loved you so much that I took up the cross of salvation. I love you. Please realize that I am talking to you here. To My death I loved you. Oh, how I love you!

3. Jesus Falls the First Time

Jesus: The cross was so heavy I could hardly walk. I held on to My cross for greatest love of you and in compliance with the Will of My Father. It became so hard to walk! The cross was so heavy! I fell. I fell and the cross fell on Me. They poked at Me, they struck Me, they demanded I get up. The pain from the instruments they used to poke Me and strike Me was so great! I somehow managed to get up.

When you fall under the weight of your cross, come to My Eucharistic Heart. I am no less present in the tabernacle and in the Eucharist than on the day I carried My cross. I wait with the same love that I had for you when I carried this cross and suffered such agony. Oh, how I love you!

4. Jesus and Mary Meet

Jesus: I saw the face of My beautiful Mother. She was weak, her face reddened and full of tears. I saw her tender heart, her love, her anguish, her pain. I saw My dear Mother Mary. My Heart was comforted by the sight of her, but torn by her suffering. **Mary:** As I looked into the eyes of my beloved Son, I saw His love. His head, bleeding and wounded. His body weak. His clothes covered with blood. I looked into His eyes and I saw His love for you. I call out to you today. I appear today with a face full of anguish and tears. I appear to call you back to the love of my Son. See through my eyes, as I peer into His eyes, the love He has for you this day to give of Himself for you. Oh, He loves you so much, my little children. See through my eyes the love of my Son. Oh, how He loves you!

5. Simon of Cyrene Is Forced to Help Jesus Carry His Cross

Jesus: The cross was so heavy I could not move. My persecutors became angry and forced a man to help Me. The cross was so heavy the two of us could barely move it. How is your cross today? Does it seem so heavy you cannot go on? I am forever watching you. When you are suffering the greatest, I am very close to you. It is in immense suffering that you realize My great love for you. Pray for grace to do always the Father's Will. Pray for grace to grow in your knowledge and love of Me.

6. Veronica Wipes the Face of Jesus

Jesus: My face was covered with blood. From the crowd Veronica came forward with a cloth to wipe My face. On the cloth I gave to you an imprint of My bloodied face. This, My children, remains with you this day as a sign of My immense love for you. But more than any cloth, look beyond the visible consecrated host. I, Jesus Christ, the Son of God, remain with you, Body, Blood, Soul and Divinity, in the Eucharist this day, waiting and longing to be with you. Oh, how I love you!

7. Jesus Falls the Second Time

Jesus: Oh, dear ones, the road became harder and harder to walk. The cross was becoming heavier, My body weaker and weaker. My shoulders and arms hurt so much! My head throbbed as I walked. The blood came from My body, from My head to My feet. I was covered with open wounds. I could not go any farther. I stumbled and fell. Again they poked at Me, only harder, and with such hatred they kicked Me. Such vileness in the hearts of men! My greatest agony was not the agonies of My body, but the agonies of My heart for the love I have for all My precious souls. I loved them so dearly. I loved those who persecuted Me. Oh, how I love you!

8. Jesus Meets the Women of Jerusalem

Jesus: The women came to Me with their children, their tender hearts crying and wanting to comfort Me. I saw their love, their care. I saw the coldness of men's hearts for all time, the hatred, the anger, the sins, all the souls that, despite all of My sufferings and death, would be condemned to eternal damnation. I told the women to weep not for Me, but for themselves and their children. My greatest agonies were the agonies of My Most Sacred Heart. Oh, how I love you!

9. Jesus Falls the Third Time

Jesus: I fell hard the third time. I was so weakened I could not go on. My body collapsed under the cross from such exhaustion! My child, My child, My greatest agonies were not the wounds to the body. They were the wounds I experienced to My heart. Do you know a little more now how I love you? It is in meditating on My Passion and death that you will realize My immense love for you. When you fall, when you struggle, I give you the grace to get up. I never give you more than you can handle. Your strength will come from Me. Come to My Eucharistic Heart. I am waiting for you this day. Oh, how I love you!

10. Jesus Is Stripped of His Garments

Jesus: They took Me to the hill to crucify Me. They angrily stripped Me of My garments. They took off My clothes to whip Me. They had covered My bloody wounds with a dirty purple robe. Now, total surrender–they took off My clothes. I showed you the way to surrender, always complying with the Will of the Father. It is in living in His Will that you will have peace and joy, and life eternal some day. Oh, how I love you!

11. They Nail Him to the Cross

R. See Mary as she holds the little Baby Jesus. See her as she washes His tender hands and feet. See her now as she watches as they pound into those same hands and feet the gigantic nails that fix Jesus to the cross.

Mary: Oh, my dear ones, my heart was torn in my chest as they nailed His hands and feet to the cross. I ask you this day to walk the Passion with me and see through my eyes the love He has for you. He truly was nailed to the cross.

Jesus: They pounded the nails into My first hand, then they stretched My body and nailed My other hand. The blood poured from these wounds that went totally through My hands. My pain was so immense, but then they nailed My feet! You do not know what pain I suffered, My child. My children, My children, for each one of you I suffered this pain. Oh, how I loved you!

12. Jesus Dies on the Cross

(Silence.)

R. He hung for three agonizing hours on the cross against the darkened sky. His greatest agonies were not the agonies of His body, but those of His Heart for the great love He has for each and every soul.

Jesus: I gave Myself to you, My dear ones. I gave My all. I hung with My arms spread in total surrender. My head was punctured; My hands and feet were nailed to the cross. I gave Myself to you. I give Myself to you this day in the Eucharist. I give Myself to you. I, God, give you Myself! What more do you want?

Song: Oh, burning Heart, oh, Love divine, etc.

R. They pierced His Heart with a lance and what flowed forth was blood and water, the sacramental life of the Church, water for Baptism and blood for the Eucharist. His life, death and resurrection live on in the Church this day.

13. Jesus Is Taken Down from the Cross and Placed in the Arms of His Mother

R. His totally lifeless body was placed in the arms of His most loving Mother. As she had held the little baby body in her arms, she now received His bloodied, bruised body in her arms. This is how He obeyed the Father's Will. Jesus gave His life for us. The Father gave His only Son because He loves us so much. Mary, His Mother, our Mother and the Mother of the Church, is forever by His side. See Jesus in the arms of His loving Mother under the cross. This is love.

Mary: I held His lifeless body in my arms. See through my eyes the love He has for you this day. He gives Himself to you today in the Eucharist. He loves you so much!

14. Jesus Is Locked in the Tomb

R. His enemies rolled the stone up to the tomb and were pleased to have buried Jesus. Mary, outside the tomb, wept bitterly. The cold reality that He was dead! But death has no power over Jesus for on the third day He rose, triumphant, from the tomb! We are partakers in His divine life. Death has no power over Jesus. He is with us this day. He comes to bring us life to the full. He loves us so much!

THE SEVEN SORROWS OF THE BLESSED VIRGIN MARY
FEBRUARY 22, 1995

1. The Prophecy of Simeon

Mary, Joseph and the child Jesus went to the temple. Simeon, the prophet, inspired by the Holy Spirit, met them and told Joseph and Mary of the great sufferings of Jesus and Mary. He told Mary that a sword would pierce her heart. From that point on, Mary ever remembered the prophecy of Simeon whenever she beheld her child. When she looked at His little body, even as an infant, she knew He would suffer. Every time she clothed Him and watched Him at play, her heart was torn in her chest as she knew what He would suffer. And a sword, too, shall pierce your Heart, O Mary!

2. The Flight into Egypt

Joseph was told by the angel to flee. Joseph, Mary and the child Jesus had to flee because of what might happen to Jesus. They had to pack for a long stay. The child Jesus was so small! They left on their journey, hearts full of fear, trying to protect Jesus. They were forced to flee into Egypt.

3. Jesus Is Lost, In the Temple

Imagine the sufferings in Mary's heart when she realized the child Jesus was not with them. Think of how it would be to lose your child and not know where he was or if anything happened to him. With sorrow in their hearts, Mary and Joseph returned to Jerusalem to look for the child Jesus. And a sword, too, shall pierce your heart, O Mary!

4. Jesus Carries His Cross

Song: See the eyes that look at Mary, her tender infant child. See the child's Heart beat so tenderly, the Savior of the world! See the eyes of Jesus and Mary as they met on Calvary. Mary's Heart knew Jesus' Heart so well! From the first moment of conception and throughout His life, Mary was so connected with Jesus and now she peered into His eyes. The crown of thorns adorned His Head! Blood ran down His face! A heavy cross on His back! Wounded, His whole body covered with bleeding wounds! And her whole life flashed before her, the life that she had spent with Jesus. This was the beloved child that she had held in her arms when Simeon told Mary that 'a sword, too, shall pierce your Heart, O Mary!'

5. Jesus Dies on the Cross

Mary stood under Jesus' cross as He was put to death. The child that she had held in her arms as Simeon prophesied, And a sword, too, shall pierce your Heart, O Mary! Now Jesus is dead on the cross! He gave His flesh, He gave His blood so that we might be with Him forever in heaven. He held not back. He gave His all. He calls out to us this day to see through the eyes of His mother as she appears and calls out with a Heart of great love, "Return to the love of my Son! He is with you this day. He remains with you, no less present than the day that He hung on the cross, in the Eucharist. He longs for you to come and be with Him. He is in your brother. How can you not love your brother when Jesus died for your brother?"

Her Heart was pierced with a sword. His Heart was pierced with a lance. What came forth was blood and water, the sacramental life of the church. He lives with us this day in the Church. He gives to us His sacraments, the source of His life! He gives to us the Sacrament of Penance whereby any sin that we commit can be taken away through the priest. He wants us to be so close to Him! He gives us everything to be close to Him. But we see with such limited vision only those things that are right before our face, when the true reality is that which we don't see with our eyes, the reality of the invisible divinity of Jesus Christ, the Son of God, in the consecrated Host! This is reality! This is our life! This is our power! This is God! And a sword, too, shall pierce your Heart, O Mary!

6. Jesus Is Taken Down from the Cross

If we ever doubted for one second that we were loved, we could visualize the picture of Mary as she sat beneath the cross with the lifeless, battered, bruised and bloodied body of her Son in her arms, the same child that she held when Simeon prophesied her suffering. He gave His last breath. He gave the last beat of His Heart. He gave His all! This is the way He complied with the Will of the Father. He came to show us the way. He died in perfect peace. To His death He was in peace because He knew the Father's love. The Father loves us so much that He gave His only begotten Son for love of us! The Spirit descended upon the Virgin Mary and the Word was made flesh! The love of the Two Hearts! Such immense love beating for us!

In all love there is suffering. Her Heart was pierced with a sword. His Heart was pierced with a lance. And a sword, too, shall pierce your Heart, O Mary!

7. Jesus Is Locked in the Tomb

And now Jesus, His body lifeless, is locked in a tomb! What cold reality for Mary to realize that His body is now gone! A stone separated her from her Son!

He gave His last breath! He gave the last beat of His Heart for love of each one of us! And she comes to us this day with her sweet, beautiful voice and she asks us to go to her Son and love Him! How can we refuse Jesus who spread His arms and gave His life for each and every one of us? How can we not trust Him when He loved us so much that He allowed them to tear His flesh, to crown Him with piercing thorns and, lastly, to hang Him on a cross? He truly gave His life for us! He, truly God, is with us this day, the same as the day He died on the cross, in the tabernacle! And we take it so lightly! Death has no power over Him! Locked in the tomb for three days, He rose triumphant on the third day as He had foretold. He comes to give us life. He gives us the sacrament of Baptism that initiates us into His life, that makes us children of God and heirs of heaven if we remain in the state of grace. He asks two things: love of God and love of one another! He came to show us the way and His way is love. To His death on the cross He loved each one of us! He calls out to each one of us here today to be His soldiers, to march on a world that has forgotten God, that has forgotten what it is like to love! It is a battle to live in this world. But the battle is won with hearts that are filled with His love, empowered by the grace and might that He pours out in the Eucharist. He calls out for us to come to the Eucharist and to the tabernacle and be fed with His very flesh and blood. To feed on Divine Life, the greatest nourishment, the Body and Blood of Jesus Christ, the Son of God! This is the love He gives. This is the love He asks us to share.

ROSARY MEDITATIONS
FEBRUARY 22, 1995
THE GLORIOUS MYSTERIES

The Resurrection

1. On the third day, Jesus rose from the dead as He had foretold. Death has no power over Him!
2. They had rolled the heavy stone in front of the tomb and His enemies believed that they had won. Jesus was locked in the tomb! These are truly the Glorious Mysteries for He rose triumphant on the third day!
3. Mary Magdalene and some of the others went to the tomb. When they arrived, they saw the stone had been rolled back.
4. Come Holy Spirit, fill us with the fire of Your love. Pour out to us Your Divine Love, Your Divine Life, so that we may partake more and more in this life and be raised to eternal life in heaven.
5. Jesus walked with two disciples on the way to Emmaus and recounted for them all the scriptures in the Old Testament from the time of Moses that referred to Him.
6. They did not understand that Jesus would die and then rise again. They did not recognize Him after He rose. You might think, 'oh, so blind were they! How could they not recognize Jesus?' But Jesus is in our midst this day. He is present right here with us. He is present in the tabernacle. He is present in us and in our world and the world continues to go on its way in blindness.
7. Take the blinders from our eyes so that we may see more and more with the vision of God. As we unite with You, lead us ever closer to the vision of God.
8. He gives us sufferings. He gives us trials. He allows all that happens to us to happen. It is in acceptance of all that He allows, and in focusing on Jesus, that we will have new life, new life in Him! He is forever present and forever ready to pour out to us His life in abundance. But we must realize that the way to Him is to follow Him. He came to carry His cross. He suffered and died so He could bring us new life!

9. *Song:* I know Your love a little now, so dear You are to me. Come give me life, abundant life, I thirst to be with Thee.

10. Who are we that God loves us so much that He sent His only Son into this world and His Son died on the cross for our redemption? Now He rises on the third day to bring us new life. He gives to the apostles the power to baptize and to forgive sins. It is through baptism that we are made children of God and heirs of heaven. We are given new life in baptism!

    We are on a spiritual journey. We are reborn in baptism as little babies on our journey, and our mother is our Spiritual Mother to lead us on our way to closer and closer union with Jesus, her beloved Son!

    Song between decades: Come Holy Spirit, fill our hearts. Enkindle in us the fire of Your love. Come, Holy Spirit, fill our…

The Ascension

1. Jesus took the apostles out to the town of Bethany and gave them His final blessing and left them in His peace. The ways of God are the ways of peace. The more we realize the immense love that the Father, Son and Holy Spirit have for us, that the three Persons are truly inside of us when we are in the state of grace, the more we then realize that no one can take away this indwelling of the Trinity within us. The more we pray and stay connected to Them, the more They lead us to peace. Peace, joy and happiness come from the realization of the presence of God within us!

2. We walk this barren land not alone. We walk with the presence of the Trinity inside of us. We are temples of the Holy Spirit. It is in the realization of this divine gift that we are given that we will have peace within. As we look at Jesus all though the passion, the look of peace is always on His face, even though He suffers, because He knows the Father's love.

3. Satan tries to distract us, tries to make us think ill thoughts. It is only in trusting God, in turning over entirely to Him our wills, our lives, our whole being, that we can have peace. It is in living in the Father's Will, in doing what He calls us to do, that we will have true happiness and peace.

4. These are the Glorious Mysteries! Jesus truly rose from the dead! Can we even comprehend that a person who died could

rise from the dead? This alone shows the magnificence of God's might!

5. And the glories that followed! He raised His arms and ascended upward into the clouds. The apostles, as they looked from below, were awestruck to see Jesus go upward into the sky, into a cloud which took Him out of sight!

6. They who walked and talked with Jesus, who were by His side, were filled with fear. As they were filled with fear, we should be gentle with ourselves when we are full of fear inside. We should realize that it was only through the power of the Spirit that they were transformed from fear to fearlessness. Almighty God can take us from the depths of doom and raise us to such immense heights, but it takes our will of surrendering to Him, of focusing on Him, of doing always the Father's Will, of living in the Father's Will as children who are being obedient to their Father.

7. *Song:* I come to you with greatest love, I am your loving Savior. I am your God, I died for you. I come to you this day.

    Nothing feeds the hungry soul but the love and the life of God!

8. He came to give us life. He nourishes this life with the Eucharist. This is Jesus truly present in His divinity and humanity. He feeds our life through His own flesh and blood! He feeds our life in Him through the divine love that He has left with us. He feeds this life through the Church, through the sacraments. He gives us the sacrament of penance whereby all our sins can be taken away through the power of the priest. God is so good to us that He truly feeds our life in Him!

9. *Song:* I Am the Bread of Life. He who comes to Me shall not hunger. He who believes in Me shall never thirst.

10. He, God, lets us partake in His divine life, in His divine love, and He nourishes us with His very own flesh and blood!

    Song between decades: Come, Holy Spirit, fill…

The Descent of the Holy Spirit

1. The apostles were full of fear and they locked themselves in the Upper Room. Jesus had told them that they would be baptized by the Holy Spirit.

2. They were locked in the Upper room with the Virgin Mary and there appeared over their heads parted tongues of fire and the Holy Spirit descended upon them. Mary is the mother of the

Church. She is our spiritual mother. She is the mother of Christ!

3. Mary is our model. She is the spouse of the Holy Spirit. It is in modeling ourselves after Mary that we become more and more like Jesus. Mary, help us to love you, to be drawn ever closer to you. Dear Spirit, please transform us in the Heart of Mary into the image of Jesus so that we may be ever closer to our beloved Father.

4. It is through Mary's pure and tender Heart that the Spirit transforms us more and more into the image of Jesus!

5. Dear Spirit, give us courage to go out into this world and preach the Gospel as did the apostles, who were filled with such fearlessness. These were the same men who, out of great fear, had locked themselves in the Upper Room. The key is the Spirit! Transform us, Spirit, please! Give us the courage to do what the Father is asking us to do: to help carry out the Gospel to the world, to help to spread the love of Jesus!

6. Please outpour Your Spirit onto this Center. Please let this Spirit dwell in us!

7. Let those involved in Our Lady of Light Ministries and the Shepherds of Christ Ministries be filled with the Spirit so that it is the Spirit that moves in them, that draws them ever closer to the Eucharistic Heart of Jesus Christ, the Son of God!

8. Transform all who are here to have the courage to carry out the worldwide plan that the Father has set before us. He Who has chosen us to be the Apostles of the Sacred Heart, to go into this world to spread the love of Jesus' burning Heart. May the Spirit move in each and every soul and draw souls ever closer to the Eucharist. For the power is truly in the Eucharistic Heart of Jesus Christ, the Son of God!

9. *Song:* Come Holy Ghost, Creator blest, and in our hearts take up Thy rest. Come with Thy grace and heavenly aid, to fill the hearts which Thou hast made, to fill the hearts which Thou hast made.

10. And He gave to them the Eucharist to feed the life that He had imparted to them, and the Spirit moved within their souls to lead them ever closer to the love of God so that this love could radiate from their being and be seen in the world.

Song between decades: Come, Holy Spirit, fill our…

The Assumption of Mary into Heaven

1. Mary was taken up into heaven, body and soul!
2. But she remains with us this day. She is our spiritual mother. She is the mother of the Church. Jesus is alive in the Church today.
3. Oh, how our mother is so much with us this very day!
4. Dear Mary, hold in your Heart all the especially anointed priests of your Son, Jesus. Hold them in your Heart and, through the Holy Spirit, lead them ever closer to the Eucharistic Heart of your Son, Jesus.
5. It is through the pierced Heart of your Son that the sacramental life of the Church was born—through the water, which represents baptism, and the blood, which represents the Eucharist. We are given life and we are fed. Hold the Church, and all those who minister there, in your Heart. Hold them ever close to you for you are their mother. Mother the Church! Hold them so close to you! Guide them! Protect them! Lead them through your spouse, the Holy Spirit, filled with the fire of God's love, into this world in which the Sacred Heart of Jesus will reign and the Immaculate Heart of Mary will be triumphant!
6. Help us in the Shepherds of Christ to carry out whatever is the Father's plan for renewing the Church, for spreading the love of His Most Sacred Heart to many people in the nursing homes, in the prisons, throughout the world. Give us the courage through the Holy Spirit to spread the love of the Two Hearts in this world that is in darkness.
7. Dear Mary, help the priests, your beloved priest-sons, to realize the great mission to which the Father has called them. Help them to lead the flock to the Eucharistic Heart of Jesus Christ.
8. Help us to be proud to be a part of your Church, to be a part of the living Body of Christ alive in this world today.
9. The Church is the Body of Christ. He is the head and we are the members. We are all one in this Body of Christ. Unite us ever closer with you, Mary, mother of the Church. Lead all in the Church to the most burning love of the Eucharistic Heart of Jesus Christ, the Son of God!
10. Oh no! Mary has not left! She is truly here in our midst! She is mothering us and she is mothering the Church!

Song between decades: Come, Holy Spirit, fill our hearts…

The Coronation of Mary as Queen of Heaven and Earth

1. There appeared in the sky a woman, clothed with the sun. The moon was under her feet and there were twelve stars about her head.

2. Mary is Queen of Heaven and Earth! The Sacred Heart of Jesus will reign and the Immaculate Heart of Mary will triumph on this earth!

3. There will be an era of peace. Peace is only found in God and in doing His Will. We must turn our hearts back to God, follow the Ten Commandments, do all that He is asking us to do, say we are sorry for our sins and draw our hearts into union with the Sacred Heart of Jesus.

4. We are the children of the Father! Jesus loved us so much that He gave His very life for us. We are the favored children created uniquely by the Father and He cares for us this day with great love. Lead us ever closer to union with the Father, the Son and the Holy Spirit through the Immaculate Heart of our mother Mary!

5. *Song:* Hail, holy queen enthroned above, O Maria! Hail, mother of mercy and of love, O Maria! Triumph, all ye Cherubim! Sing with us, ye Seraphim! Heaven and earth resound the hymn, Salve, salve, salve, Regina!

6. All souls are joined in the Church with the souls in purgatory and with the angels and saints in heaven. We are all one in His Body. Let us love God, for we are children of God. We are brothers in Christ!

7. Help us to see more and more the big picture. Help us to let go of little details and see more with the vision of God all that we need to see to do His work here on this earth—to let go of the little daily distractions, but to see that we are His soldiers marching on a world that is godless. Help us to realize that souls are at stake and that Mary and Jesus are calling us to be these soldiers to spread His love.

8. Who are we that God is so good to us?

9. Mary, our Queen, lead us ever closer to Jesus' Heart. Be with us as we walk with Jesus on Calvary. Be with us and lead us to everlasting life so that we may one day be united with the Father, Son and Holy Spirit forever and ever.

10. May the saints and angels guide us on our way to eternal salvation.

May we know God more and more. May He outpour His love on us, His beloved ones. We are His and He loves us so much!

Song after last decade: Come Holy Spirit, fill our hearts...

Song: Holy God, we praise Thy name. Lord of all, we bow before Thee. All on earth Thy scepter claim. All in heaven above adore Thee. Infinite, Thy vast domain, everlasting is Thy reign. Infinite Thy vast domain, everlasting is Thy reign!

ROSARY MEDITATIONS
MARCH 1, 1995
THE SORROWFUL MYSTERIES

The Agony in the Garden

1. **Jesus:** Surrender! Surrender to Me as I surrendered to the Father in the Garden. I said to My Father, "Nevertheless, let your will be done, not mine." (Lk 22:42) As you are in your hearts troubled and anxious, I am there ever present to comfort you, to give you My peace. Let go, let go, let go! I am forever with you at every second, at every moment. I do not go! I forever remain in your hearts. Let go! As you live, so do I live in you!

2. **Jesus:** I knelt in the Garden in such agony! I saw before Me all that I would undergo, all the beatings, all the scourging. I knew the Father's Will. I complied with the Father's Will as I ask you to surrender totally to Me. Let go! Focus on Me! Do not focus on those things that are parading in your mind, but release your mind to the mysteries of heaven, to My Passion and My death!

3. **Jesus:** And My faithful ones, who came to comfort Me—they slept!

4. **Jesus:** Indifference! Ingratitude! Neglect! I saw before Me all those who would neglect Me and treat Me with indifference. How My Heart ached with pain to see the souls that I loved so dearly filled with such nonsense!

5. **Jesus:** My Heart, an endless furnace of divine love, of divine life, beating and burning for love of precious souls and they do not see! They have closed their eyes and plugged up their ears and I wait and long to be ever close to them! Spread My love

throughout this world. You will be met with resistance on all sides. But I beg you this day to listen to My cry. I cry out to you to stand firm. I am calling you to stand up against the world.

6. **Jesus:** As one crying in the wilderness, prepare the way of the Lord. I cry out to you to go to the highways and byways. Shout from the rooftops that I am Lord and that I am in your midst this day. Prepare Me a way, for I am coming!

7. **Jesus:** I saw before Me all the souls that would be lost to eternal damnation despite all My sufferings. I call out to you this day to harken to My pleading to be about this world spreading My love. There are souls that are at stake, depending upon what you do with your lives. Will you spread My love? Will you be My mouthpiece to this world? I call out to you. You must stand strong and pray to the Spirit for He transforms you from fear to fearlessness. You are My apostles to go into this world and spread the love of My Most Sacred Heart!

8. **Jesus:** As I knelt in the Garden, as I suffered so many agonies in My Heart, I was comforted by the love that you show to Me this day.

9. *Song:* O Burning Heart, O Love divine! How sweet You are to me. I see the Host, I know You are here, to love and care for me.

10. **Jesus:** The world is blind and deaf! They have plugged up their ears and covered their eyes. You must go into this world. You must stand strong. You have a message of My love to give. I beg you to give this message to the world that is in much pain, that has covered its eyes and plugged up its ears. I beg you to spread this love in every corner of this world this day. You are apostles that I send into this world.

Song between decades: I come to you with greatest love. I am your loving Savior. I am your God. I died for you. I come to you this day.

Jesus Is Scourged at the Pillar

1. **Jesus:** The blood that I shed when I was scourged was blood red! My Heart, which beats out of endless love for you, is a Heart that is red, beating with a burning fire for love of you. I call out to you to draw yourselves ever closer to My Heart for I am waiting and longing and thirsting for your love. Let go of the little distractions you have this day that keep you from increased union with Me. Release yourself and be totally alone

in deep union with Me. See only Me. Let go. Release yourselves! I am here with You!

2. **Jesus:** Totally focus on Me!

3. **Jesus:** Release yourself from all the distractions in your heart. Be alone in deep union with Me!

4. **Jesus:** Just as I shed My blood for you as they scourged Me, My Heart cries this day in endless love.

5. **Jesus:** See them as they beat Me at the pillar. Hear the blows! This is the love that I have for you. This day will you be alone with Me and totally focus on only Me? Let yourself go. Be in a room where we are together in close union.

6. **Jesus:** And our hearts beat so closely, as one!

7. Hail Mary . . .

8. **Jesus:** See Me at the pillar! See Me as I stand with the deepest love for all souls.

9. *Song:* Come unto Me all who are weary and find rest for your souls. Come unto Me, all who are burdened. I will comfort you.

   Jesus: I am with you in deep union despite the distractions and all that goes on around you. I am so closely connected with you! Your concentration on Me is important to your union with Me. Focus totally on My beating Heart and the love that I have for you. My Heart beats with deep love as I stood at the pillar and bled dark red blood.

10. **Jesus:** It is this blood I shed for you, this blood I gave for you, that I ask you to focus on this day. Think of what it is like to shed your blood for another person. Would you shed your blood for another person? I shed My blood for you. In meditating on this blood that I shed, you will realize more and more the immensity of My love.

    Song between decades: I come to you with greatest love . . .

Jesus Is Crowned with a Crown of Thorns

1. **Jesus:** I come to talk to you to tell you the desires of My Heart. As people are blind and do not see, I talk to you this day and ask you to focus on Me and to know that I am truly with you. As you breathe and as your heart beats, I am ever present and within you. I am here present with you. I am the Almighty God! My love I outpour to you. My grace I give to you.

2. **Jesus:** I am the Almighty God! I am forever present. It is in your suffering that you are strengthened. I ask you to focus on

the crown of thorns they placed on My head. As the blood ran down the sides of My face, think of how this felt! As I sat wounded, My body covered with deep wounds and bleeding, the blood ran into My eyes and into My ears. This is the blood that I shed for you.

3. **Jesus:** Put yourself there as I sit. Feel as they spit on Me! Feel as they poke at Me! Think of how you would feel to be treated the way they treated Me! Put yourself on the chair and go through My sufferings with Me.

4. **Jesus:** Feel your head as it pounds from the thorns! Feel the blood as it runs on your body! Feel the gashes that burn so deeply under the cloak! Feel the spit as it hits your face! This is the love that I have for you!

5. **Jesus:** I ask you to be My soldiers, to go out into this world. They persecuted Me. They whipped Me. They crowned Me with thorns and they put Me to death. I loved those who treated Me so violently. I ask you this day to focus entirely on Me. If the earth falls down around you, interiorly the Father, Son and Holy Spirit are forever within your breast with such love.

6. **Jesus:** No person can ever take away your union within with the Father, Son and Holy Spirit. Your union forever and ever and ever in eternity depends upon the union you have with God here.

7. **Jesus:** I call you to sainthood! I call you to holiness! As I suffered this spit that hit My face and body, I call you to suffer with Me all the persecution that you may receive. For in this persecution I am totally present at every second. As your heart beats, as you breathe every breath, I never leave you! If the earth shakes around you, if it rocks and the floor cracks, you will sit steadfast for I never leave you. Hear the small, gentle voice within your heart as it calls to you, "I love you, I love you, I love you!"

8. **Jesus:** My Heart is bleeding from the indifference I receive in this world. I call out to you to be strong soldiers. You must focus on Me and this interior committedness to Me.

9. Hail Mary . . .

10. *Song:* Crown Him with many crowns, the Lamb upon His throne. His regal scepter knows no bounds. All kingdoms are His own. All Christians come and sing to Him who died for Thee. And hail Him as our Saviour King for all eternity.

Song between decades: I come to you with greatest love . . .

Jesus Carries His Cross Up Calvary

1. **Jesus:** Hear the still, small voice as it says so gently inside: "I love you, I love you, I love you!"

2. **Jesus:** I ask you to carry your crosses as I carried Mine. The cross was so heavy I could scarcely move. I fell under its weight. I ask you to accept your crosses willingly. It is in accepting these crosses that you will be strengthened for I provide everything you need. Your lessons I teach you with the greatest love. Your crosses I give you out of great love for you. It is in these crosses that you receive new life, new life in Me! Accept all that I give you!

3. **Jesus:** As I walked with My cross on My back, I peered into the beloved eyes of My dear Mother. Her face was reddened! The tears from her eyes! I could see the sufferings deep within far more than the features of her face. How My Heart was torn to see My beloved Mother, whom I love so much, riddled with such suffering!

4. **Jesus:** I watch you, My child. I am forever with you! I know all the desires, the sufferings, of your heart. It is in your sufferings, your acceptance of your sufferings, that you give Me such great love.

5. **Jesus:** How do you love Me, child? You love Me through holiness, through loving your brothers. Always love! I loved those who persecuted Me. You must always love! Focus on the love I have for you and hear the still, small voice as it whispers within your heart: "I love you, I love you, I love you!"

6. **Jesus:** You are My beloved ones. You I love. You I want closer union with. You, you, My precious loved ones!

7. **Jesus:** Carry the crosses that I give to you with great joy, for they are given to you with My great love. It is in carrying these crosses that you will receive new life in Me.

8. **Jesus:** I was crowned with thorns! I was beaten over My entire body! I was always at peace. Remain at peace for you know the immense love that I have for you. I never leave you.

9. **Jesus:** It is in following the Father's Will and living in His Will as a little child that you will have peace, joy and true happiness.

10. **Jesus:** My dear soldiers, you are being strengthened for the days ahead. I am totally with you and present. All that you undergo I am allowing. I ask you to accept each and every suffering that I give you as a gift from Me to you, given out of great love! It is

in these sufferings that you will be drawn ever closer to My Most Sacred Heart.

Song between decades: I come to you with greatest love...)

Jesus Dies on the Cross

1. **Jesus:** I hung for three agonizing hours to My death on the cross! Put yourself on the cross. Your hands nailed, your feet nailed to the cross! Your body covered with wounds! Put yourself there!

2. **Jesus:** It is in meditating on My passion that you will know of My immense love.

3. **Jesus:** I truly hung there to My death!

4. **Jesus:** I accepted death on the cross in compliance with My Father's Will and in great love for you.

5. *Song:* I come to you with greatest love. I am your loving Savior. I am your God. I died for you. I come to you this day.

6. **Jesus:** This is the love that I have for you this day. I ask you to put the world aside. Focus on loving one another. Focus on Me! I fill you with this immense love. Hear the cry of the voice inside: "I love you, I love you." Do not be angry with those around you. It is your committedness to Me, committedness to this union with Me, to making Me the center of your every thought, to letting Me live in you, through you and with you, and at every second to totally surrender, that allows Me to operate in you. It is no longer you who live, but I who live in you!

7. **Jesus:** You are My chosen ones, to whom I give My Heart!

8. **Jesus:** My Heart was pierced with a lance and what poured out was the abounding love from My Heart, blood and water for your salvation!

9. **Jesus:** It is up to you to let go! Always love! I loved those who persecuted Me. I did not hold grudges. I loved. There is no division in love. There is always unity in love. You must love all! I loved those who put Me to death! I surrendered always to the Father's Will. Anything that happens to you this day I am allowing! Accept what I am giving to you today and love it as coming from Me.

10. **Jesus:** Among the thorns there will be a bed of roses. Come to My bed of roses!

Song after the last decade: I come to you with greatest love...

ROSARY MEDITATIONS
MARCH 17, 1995 NOON
THE SORROWFUL MYSTERIES

Every Friday at Noon, Jesus gave us a very tender rosary. We always did the Sorrowful Mysteries on Friday at 12:00 noon. This was the first rosary received in the Sorrowful Mother Chapel before the exposed Eucharist. Rita was in an ecstatic state. Marty saw angels around the monstrance and Sorrowful Mother statue.

The Agony in the Garden

1. **R.** Be with Jesus in the Garden, alone with Him as if you are there and experiencing what He is about to undergo. Think of knowing all that you will suffer. See before you all that He is about to experience. Put yourself with Jesus in the Garden and feel deeply in your heart whatever the Spirit allows you to experience.

2. **Jesus:** I am an endless furnace of love. My Heart is beating for each one of you here. See My Heart as it beats. Think of this beating. Think of the beating Heart!

3. **Jesus:** I pour out to you My endless love constantly. I never leave you. I am forever with you, second by second, minute by minute. I am forever present with you in this room the same as the day I knelt in the Garden. Be alone with Me. Empty your mind of any distractions, of any concerns. Be totally wrapped in the love that I am giving to you. Open your hearts wide and let Me unite ever so closely within your heart. I am Jesus, your most ardent Lover, on fire for love of you, My beloved ones. As I knelt in the Garden, I pondered the ways of your heart. My Heart ached for all the souls that would treat Me with such indifference and neglect. Comfort My aching Heart with your love for Me.

4. **Jesus:** Be with Me as I kneel and see all of the sufferings that I experience. But the sufferings that I experienced to My body were not My greatest sufferings. My greatest sufferings were the agonies that I experienced in My Heart for the endless souls that pay Me no heed, that never come to Me, that stay at such a distance. And I am in love with them, so deeply in love!

5. **Jesus:** I call out to you to take My plea seriously. My plea involves the salvation of souls. Open your hearts and let Me unite

closely to you so that I can live in you. Through you I will touch My beloved ones that I love so dearly. How I love you this day, My precious ones. Be alone with Me, totally wrapped in My embrace. I am Jesus, your Savior, and I love you with the deepest, tenderest love. I pour My love out to you. Harken to Me. Let go!

6. Hail Mary . . .

7. Hail Mary . . .

8. **Jesus:** Surrender! Surrender! Surrender! Open wide the gates to your hearts. You are so closed. You tap at My source so lightly when I am an ocean of endless love and mercy that I want to pour into your hearts. You must surrender to become closely united to Me. You think you are letting go. You are not letting go! You are holding on as tightly as you can hold on. You let go of what you want to let go of. I am calling you to more, to be so closely united that I can operate through you. Will you surrender or will you control everything that is in your life that pertains to Me? I want to live with you second by second, to operate in every deed that you do, to be one with you as you perform those deeds. You are My mighty soldiers to go into the war and to do My work. Surrender! Surrender! Surrender!

9. **Jesus:** Open wide the portals of your heart. Let me penetrate every cell of your being. I want such oneness with you. You do not comprehend My immense love. You must surrender!

10. **Jesus:** Consecrate yourself totally to My Heart and that of My Mother.

Song between decades: I come to you with greatest love, I am your loving Savior. I am your God, I died for you. I come to you this day.

Jesus Is Scourged at the Pillar

1. **R.** His body was beaten! His flesh was torn! He was scourged and bleeding!

2. **R.** He stood in total surrender to His persecutors. He knew the Father's Will. He knew the plan of salvation, that He was dying for the salvation of all.

3. **R.** He stood in such total submission to these men who treated Him so harshly. He did not answer back, always in compliance with the Father's Will. It is in compliance with His Will that our peace and joy lie. He has a plan for each one of us, His specially loved children.

4. **Jesus:** They whipped Me! They tore My flesh! They treated Me with such harshness. I withstood all of this treatment. But the greatest agonies were not the agonies of My body but the agonies in My Most Sacred Heart for all the souls in their busy lives that have totally forgotten Me. I am in your midst and with you this very day and how many come to be with Me? A few! So big is this world and so few even realize that I am God and that I am truly present here with you!

5. **Jesus:** They will persecute you! They will treat you with such anger! Come to My Heart and know the immensity of My love. For, minute by minute, second by second, I am ever attentive to all of your needs. I am the most ardent Lover, waiting to be close to you. If you tap ever so gently, there is so much more!

6. **Jesus:** I pour My life out to you. My grace is My life. It is divine life that I give. Nothing on this earth compares to this divine life!

7. **Jesus:** Pray to be sensitive to My touch. Every time that I give you My grace I am touching you in a special way so that you may respond to all the graces that I am pouring out to you this day.

8. **Jesus:** I give to you My Heart as a sign of My immense love for you. See My Heart beating! See it, each pulse of My Heart! This is how I love you. Second by second, minute by minute, I am always there.

9. **Jesus:** I want to be one in you, to operate from you! You must surrender!

10. Hail Mary…

Song between decades: I come to you with greatest love…

Jesus Is Crowned with a Crown of Thorns

1. **R.** They pounded into His head a crown of sharp, piercing thorns.

2. **R.** Think of how it would be to have someone pound into your head thorns that would puncture your skull. The blood ran from these thorns down His face, into His eyes and into His ears.

3. **R.** He had seen before Him in the Garden all of these things that they would do. Now He experienced exactly what He had seen. At any time, He could have stopped anything that happened because He was God! But because He loves each one of us with the deepest love, He allowed them to pound into His skull sharp, piercing thorns that punctured His head. He

allowed them to beat Him and tear His flesh. He stood in total submission to the Will of the Father, His Heart ever beating, as it beats for us this day, with deepest love. The same Jesus that suffered this agony loves us with this same love this day. So many do not even think of Him. How His Heart was wounded and hurt for all His beloved ones!

4. **R.** This is Jesus Christ. He is truly God! God took the form of a human being because He loved us so much. He took on our human nature. A divine person took on our human form!

5. **R.** Who are we that God loves us this much?

6. **R.** They spit on Him and they hollered obscenities at Him. Think of the things that irritate us this day. Even when people are not cruel to us, how we ponder in our minds things that we think someone may have done that might have been cruel! But Jesus came to show us the way. They pounded into His Head a crown of sharp, piercing thorns and He loves those who did this to Him. He asks us to love one another. His way is always love. He asks us to purify our hearts, not to give in to the ways of the mind, not to give in to thinking ill thoughts of our brothers, but to purify our hearts and focus on Him. His way is love, always love, not sizing up our brothers or ever thinking harshly of them. See them through His eyes, the eyes of love. See our brothers as the creation of our Father. How He loves each and every soul that He was beaten, that His flesh was torn, that He was crowned with thorns because He loves our brothers so much.

7. **Jesus:** I want to tell each one of you this day of My immense love that I have for you. You do not realize how I am truly speaking here to you. You close your hearts. You cut yourself off from the grace I am giving to you. I truly love with the deepest love. Open up your hearts and surrender. My ways are so simple. My ways are truth! You must release yourselves and come to Me for all your needs. Realize that, minute by minute, second by second, I am dealing with you directly.

8. **Jesus:** The very hairs of your head are numbered. I am with you at this second and I am providing for every one of your cares and needs but your minds are busy and you think of all that you must do. When will you release yourself and let Me operate with you in every deed that you do? When will you become

one with Me so that I can operate through you to do the work that is at hand? You are humans. When I become one with you, the might of God is within you. I can do in one second what a human cannot do in a million years. You must trust. You must surrender. You must let go. Let go now and be totally wrapped in My love, My intense love that I pour out to you, My beloved ones. Let go! Let go! Let go, for I am truly here and working in your heart.

9. *Song:* Crown Him with many crowns, the Lamb upon His throne. His regal scepter knows no bounds, all kingdoms are His own. All Christians come and sing to Him Who died for thee and hail Him as thy Savior King for all eternity.

10. Hail Mary...

Song between decades: I come to you with greatest love...

Jesus Carries His Cross

1. **Jesus:** They gave Me a heavy cross that they placed on My shoulder and I carried My cross. I could hardly move but My thoughts were always of you and the immense love that I have for you.

2. **Jesus:** This world has rejected God! This world crucified Me! Why do you not realize that they will crucify you, that they will persecute you, that they will holler slanders against you? If they crucified Me, why should they treat you any differently when you spread My word?

3. **Jesus:** You are the soldiers that I send into battle, a battle to spread My love throughout this world. It is in your submissiveness and surrender that I can operate through you to give My love to this world.

4. **Jesus:** Surrender! Surrender! Surrender! I am calling out to you to take up your cross and go into battle, to battle for Me to spread this love, for souls will be lost to eternal damnation because they do not know My love.

5. **Jesus:** Time is drawing near. I tell you! I tell you! I tell you! As I spoke then, and many did not listen, I tell you today that I am depending upon you, My beloved ones. You must fight against the godlessness of this world. But you must go on. You must be My warriors that go into battle. Powered by the fire of My love, you can conquer the earth with your hearts filled with the

immense love that I pour out to this world through you. You will be the light that will shine in the darkest night. You will be a city set on a hill that will shine to the rest of this world. Come to My Heart and take refuge in My Heart for I am truly God and I call out to you, My beloved ones, with such tender love this day.

6. **Jesus:** As I walked on and on with the heavy cross on My back, a cross which became heavier as I walked, your crosses seem to get heavier each day. Time is so short! The work you do here will help you lead souls to eternal happiness in heaven. Please listen to Me! Have courage! Pray to the Spirit for the fearlessness to do the job that is at hand. I send you into this world to preach the Gospel. You are My soldiers going into battle. You will light up this world. A city set on a hill will shine to the rest of this world. You are the city. You are My soldiers. I send you into battle.

7. **Jesus:** In battle there is bloodshed. On My way to Calvary I shed much blood for love of My beloved souls. I ask you to surrender and to do this work for Me this day for I truly gave My life for love of each precious soul. Will you not spread this love to a world that is in pain and hurting?

8. **Jesus:** Surrender! Surrender! Surrender! It is not by your own might that you will light up the world. It is only through My power radiating through you. It is only in your oneness with Me. The most important thing you can do is to spend time with Me each day, to become one in Me. Keep your focus on Me and all will fall into line for I am truly here and longing to operate from your hearts. I am the Almighty God. My power is endless, My love a source of such love that no human can even comprehend. I am God! I am speaking to you!

9. Hail Mary . . .
10. Hail Mary . . .

Song between decades: I come to you with greatest love...

Jesus Is Crucified and Dies on the Cross

1. **Jesus:** I hung for three agonizing hours on the cross. My body was beaten, My head crowned with thorns. I breathed My last breath, My thoughts always of you, My beloved ones. I truly died for you.

2. **Jesus:** Do you not hear My plaintive cries, the cries that I am giving to you this day, to spread this love throughout the world? You are the backbone. You are the ones that will carry this out. You must be strong soldiers. I am speaking directly to you. You

are going into battle. It is a hard battle. Do not be discouraged by the opposition that Satan has created for you. He will try to stop you at every turn, but you must be strong soldiers and you must stayed fixed in Me. Only if you are rooted in My love can you do the work that I am asking you to do. You are human. You, on your own, cannot do this work. This work is the work of lighting up the world with the fire of My love. You must be strong soldiers. You are truly battling a world that hates God. Come to My Heart and receive all that you need to light up this world.

3. **Jesus:** My Mother stood under My cross. My beloved Mother! How she loves each one of you. Go to the Heart of Mary and reside in her arms. Rest in her Heart. This is Her House. She is with each one of you on your journey. We love you with the tenderest love.

4. **Jesus:** As she stood by Me all through My life, she stands by your side. Think of that! Where you are sitting now, Mary is right by you. Do you feel her presence? Put yourself on the other side. Be alone with Us now. Let go of this world. Be touched by the grace of God, special grace that I am giving to you alone. The angels and saints are so present here at this Center. They are in the halls. You do not realize because you do not see. You must be alone with Me and let go of your world to be united ever closer and to see these things that I want to show you.

5. **Jesus:** See Me hanging on the cross. Do you see that? Do you need to see with your eyes? Do you know what you feel when you receive the Eucharist? You must reach more and more beyond your vision. Reach into your heart. I communicate in your heart. Such oneness I have with you in your heart! See beyond your eyes, beyond your ears, and go inside into your heart. Minute by minute, second by second, I am there! Mary is with you. My Father and the Holy Spirit are inside of you. You just do not see. Pray more for grace to partake in the life I want to give you.

6. **Jesus:** Pray to the Holy Spirit to open your eyes more and more to the things of God. You are all blind men! You do not realize the great gifts that you have. You must be lost in My Heart. Come to My Heart and let Me hold you close to My divine love!

7. **Jesus:** My love is burning and on fire for you. Do you see Me as I hang on the cross with My arms outstretched? I held on to nothing! I totally surrendered to the Will of the Father. I held nothing back. I gave My flesh and My blood. I was born in poverty in a stable and I died on the cross. I came to show you the way so that you might have life and have life to the full. Life is not life if it is not rooted in Me!

8. **Jesus:** Let Me pour My life out to you. Feel its vibrancy within you. I am truly with you this day and longing for closer union with you. Let go! Let go! Let go!

9. **Jesus:** It is in this time that you spend alone with Me that I can work in your heart. Do not look for visions. Do not look to hear things. Go inside of your heart and be alone with Me. Spend this time with Me each day and, through the day, spend short periods, minutes when you just close your eyes and focus on My presence with you, for I am truly present. I will work in your heart when you come to Me in these special moments.

10. **Jesus:** This time between noon and 3:00 p.m. is so important to Me. Spend this time focusing on being ever more united to Me and think of My passion. See Me as I hung on the cross. See My flesh torn! See the blood as it ran down My body. Spend this time each Friday focused from noon until 3:00 p.m. on My passion. It is in meditating on this passion that you will realize My immense love that I have for you. I truly gave My blood. I gave you My flesh. I give you My body and I give you My blood this day in the Eucharist. Come to Me and spend time with Me after Communion and let Me work in your heart, for I love you so dearly, My beloved ones. I am Jesus. Jesus! I love you so much!

Song after the last decade: I come to you with greatest love…

ROSARY MEDITATIONS
MARCH 21, 1995
THE SORROWFUL MYSTERIES

This rosary was said by candlelight during the Tuesday Shepherds of Christ meeting. Jesus told Rita to pray this rosary in front of the Pieta statue in the back of the Rosary chapel. Rita was in an ecstatic state. Some present at the Rosary saw Jesus alive in the statue and blood running from His wounds. During the crucifixion His face was white. Mary was seen crying.

The Agony in the Garden

1. **R.** Be there with Jesus in the Garden in the darkened night as He kneels. Before Him He sees all the sufferings He is about to undergo.

2. **R.** His Heart is in such anguish to see before Him all the souls that will be lost despite all the sufferings He is about to experience.

3. **R.** We tap ever so lightly at the door of His Heart. He is an endless, burning furnace of fire, on love for each one of us. He says, "You do not know even the smallest amount of the immensity of the love that I have for you. You must come into My Heart. It is in My Heart that I lavishly give you My great love."

4. **R.** Think of the Heart of the Virgin Mary from the first moment of conception and how she carried the child within her womb, how she watched Him at play. All through His life Mary was there, to His death on the cross. How her Heart knows the Heart of Jesus! She stood under the cross. She held His lifeless body in her arms under the cross. It is through the Heart of Mary that we will more tenderly embrace the love that Jesus has for us. See Him as He kneels in the Garden, His Heart in such anguish. His sweat became as great drops of blood upon the ground. He knew all the souls that would reject this immense love that He has, who would not even care, who would go about their days without even thinking of Him. Yet He longs to be so united to each one of us so that every action we perform is an acton we do in oneness with Him. Jesus' Heart was in such anguish that His sweat became as great drops of blood on the ground.

5. **R.** Think of the mystery all through this rosary! Think of the mystery! There is a mystery when there is blood! The blood comes from deep within. Think of the mystery that Jesus sweat blood! He was in such anguish!

6. **R.** He tenderly calls to us day after day. Do we hear His gentle call, deep within our hearts, to be joined ever closer to Him? How many times do we reject the love that Jesus outpours to us because we are not sensitive to the little call that He makes to us

in our hearts. He suffered in the Garden for all the souls He loved so dearly, some of whom would reject Him totally.

7. **R.** He suffered in the Garden for all of our sins, for our haughtiness and our pride, for our lack of compassion and mercy for our brothers. Yet He gives to us unconditional love and asks us to love one another. In the Our Father we say, "Forgive us our trespasses as we forgive those…" He suffered for all the times that we say no to forgiving our brothers. We forgive some but not all and think it is okay. Jesus loves each and every soul.

8. **Jesus:** Come to My open Heart through My pierced side. Look at the wound in My side. Suffering helps you reach My immense love. Enter My Heart through My pierced side and fall deeply into the abyss of My great love.

9. **Jesus:** Do not let your hearts turn cold! You must come to Me with hearts that are soft and ready to love. Put aside all the hardness in your hearts, for a soul that is haughty and angry cannot unite with My love. I long to be in the deepest union with each one of you present. So deep! You cannot fathom the great love that I have for you. You must clean your hearts of all the debris. Sweep away the unforgiveness and come into My Heart through My pierced side.

10. **Jesus:** My Heart was in such agony that I sweat blood. Do you know, even a small amount, the immense love that I have for you? I was born a helpless baby in the town of Bethlehem and I gave My flesh and My blood for love of you.

Song between decades: I come to you with greatest love, I am your loving Savior. I am your God, I died for you. I come to you this day.

Jesus Is Scourged at the Pillar

1. **R.** Think of Jesus! Visualize Him, totally present, His body here! See Him as they lead Him away. They poke at Him! They pull His hair! See this so clearly in your mind. A person named Jesus being led away!

2. **R.** What a sight for our eyes if we truly saw what happened there, if saw them with such violence and anger tie Jesus, our friend, to the pillar and then take out weapons and beat His flesh!

3. **R.** This is your best friend, Jesus Christ. They have tied Him to a pillar and they are beating Him with instruments that are tear-

ing His flesh. The blood is pouring down His body!

4. **R.** They shout at Him and they holler angry and ugly remarks. He does not respond, only grunts as they hit Him harder. To their own exhaustion they beat Jesus. Watch this!
Jesus: It is in your heart that you will know Me, My dear children. You must visualize more and more the lives of Myself and My Mother. As you go through these mysteries of the rosary, put yourself there. See as if you were present. Experience what I went through. It is in knowing Our lives that you will know the great love that We have for you.

5. **R.** He stood in a puddle of His own blood!

6. **R.** This is my beaten friend Jesus! He shed His blood for love of me so that I may be with Him forever in heaven.

7. **R.** Hear the blows that they give to Jesus! Listen! Hear the blows! These are the blows that He suffered for love of each one of us. He suffered those blows for each and every soul, the poor beggar, the person that is a little different, the person that is not as rich as I am, the person that is somewhat short, the person that I think looks strange. Jesus stood at the pillar and was beaten for each one of these persons. These are my brothers! When Jesus came to the world, He made us brothers with God!

8. **R.** If I stood at the pillar next to you, Jesus, and they beat my back and tore my flesh, if I did it for someone here and they did not even think about me, how my heart would ache. But You are God! You, Who are infinite Love, suffered this brutal persecution for love of each one of us. How did Your Heart ache, Jesus, when You suffered Your bloodied flesh and knew that people would not even think about You?

9. **R.** And what do you ask of me, Jesus? To love God and love my brother! To become more closely united to You as You outpour divine love and divine life!

10. **Jesus:** I call you to purity. I call you to open up your hearts, to rid yourselves of anything that is impure. I long to be closely united with each of you. People are watching you! If you call yourselves Christians, then you must act as I would act! Do you preach the Gospel in your actions? Is your way the way of love? I came to show you the way. Will you follow Me? Will you love all your brothers as I ask you to do? People are watching you, My faithful Christians, apostles that I send into this world to

spread the love of My Most Sacred Heart. You are being watched and are teaching so many lessons through your example. I call out to you today to rid yourselves of all impurities in your heart. Then you will receive a reward that far surpasses anything you can gain on this earth. You will receive closer union with My Most Sacred Heart. I love you! I love you! I love you! Moment by moment, second by second, I am there to provide you with everything you need. You must surrender and trust in Me!

Song between decades: I come to you with greatest love…

Jesus Is Crowned with a Crown of Thorns

1. **Jesus:** They tore My flesh! They beat My body! I shed My blood! They pounded into My head a sharp crown of thorns that pierced My head and punctured My forehead!

2. **R.** Jesus, You bled for love of each one of us. Help us to realize during this Lenten season the immensity of Your love as we meditate on Your wounds, the wounds to Your most precious Head, the wounds that you suffered to Your hands and feet. How would it be to rub our hands across Jesus' head, to touch the puncture wounds from the thorns! He truly suffered this for love of us!

3. **R.** The thorns were pounded into His head and He bled down His face and into His hair. Think of His hair covered with blood from the thorns that punctured His head!

4. **R.** Let me kiss your wounds, dear Jesus, the wounds that you suffered for love of me! Let me enter into the wound in Your side. The more deeply I enter into this wound, the more I enter the abyss of the endless love of Your Most Sacred Heart.

5. *Song:* Crown Him with many crowns, the Lamb upon His throne. His regal scepter knows no bounds, all kingdoms are His own. All Christians come and sing to Him Who died for thee. And hail Him as our Savior King for all eternity.

6. **R.** Jesus is God! He is the King of all Kings! God took on a human nature and came into this world a helpless baby. Now He is spit upon and taunted, He is hollered at and He sits on a mockery of a throne.

7. **R.** We look for love in so many places when, minute by minute, second by second, Jesus is inside of our hearts telling us how He

is truly there and loving us.

8. **R.** If you put your fingers into the nail marks in His hands and into His side, would you believe that, minute by minute, second by second, He loves you so much, and that He is God and will provide you with all your needs?

9. *Song:* Only this I want, but to know the Lord. And to bear His cross and to wear the crown He wore.

10. **R.** Minute by minute, second by second, hear the soft, gentle voice within your heart say, "I love you, I love you, I love you. It is in realizing this immense love that there is love to give to others.

Song between decades: I come to you with greatest love…

Jesus Carries His Cross to Calvary

1. **R.** He came to serve. He came into the world in such poverty in a stable in the town of Bethlehem. He left this world hanging on a cross. Both were bare wood! He came to show us the way! Meditate on this mystery as He carries His cross. The Son of God! He took on human form for love of us. He came to show us how to love.

2. *Song:* We were made for service to care for each other. We were made to love each sister and brother. With love that will last our whole life through…

3. **R.** Jesus came and He loved and He preached the Gospel. His way was love. He always acted in love and they condemned Him to death. When we preach the Gospel, when we act from love, why do we expect people to treat us differently when they treated Jesus this way? But He came and carried His cross to show us His way and His way is the way of love. He promises to us an everlasting reward far beyond our comprehension. Look at the Virgin Mary and the Pieta. Look at her face and see through her eyes as she watches her Son, with the cross on His back, covered with blood and wounds. This is her beloved Son! Look at her face. She comes today to ask us to go into this world and to spread His love. She asks us to open up our hearts and put aside any hatred or anger that we have, for if we do not spread this love, who will spread love into this world? Open up your hearts! Be not hardened but be as Jesus has asked us to be, with hearts that are filled with love, going into battle in a world that has forgotten God. He calls us this day to be His soldiers, to

spread the fire of His love throughout the world. You may be persecuted, you may be spit on. Whatever happens, remember what they did to Him. His way is love and His reward is everlasting life.

4. **R.** These are rosaries from the Hearts of Jesus and Mary. See their eyes as they gaze at one another on the way to Calvary. Look at her face here! The horror, on top of more horror, to behold her beloved Son in such anguish! She asks us to see through her eyes the suffering that her Son endured for love of us. The more we realize the love He has, the more we will go into the world and take this love to others. We are soldiers of the Most Sacred Heart of Jesus.

5. **R.** He wants to become one with us so that it is no longer we who operate, but it is He Who operates in us, so that our every action is an action that we perform with Jesus, and the might is the might of the Almighty God within us! In order to unite this way with Him, we must be ever pure. Love unites only with love! If our hearts are filled with hatred and anger for any person, we cannot be one with Him. He longs for this love. He longs to be one in us! He wants to penetrate our souls with the fire of His love. Pray to the Spirit so that the Spirit moves inside of you.

6. **R.** See the horror in Mary's face and in her eyes. How would your face look if you were looking at your Son, covered with blood and wounded, as He fell under the cross? How would your face look? How would your heart be? It is through Mary's pure and sinless Heart that she will take us deeper and deeper into the Heart of Jesus. There is such oneness between these two Hearts, such connection between them! Look at the Pieta and see her, see her face, as she watches the Passion of her Son!

7. **R.** They hit Him on the head and the blood ran from the corners of His mouth. His face was covered with blood and Veronica wiped His face.

8. **Jesus:** My children, My children! I do not tell you things to be taken lightly. In My Heart I am longing for such union with you but you do not hear. You close your eyes and plug up your ears. You do not listen time and time again. I have come to you this evening and I have asked you to pray in front of this statue. I ask you to meditate on this. You do not know what I am saying

to you. You take these words lightly. This world is in pain. You do not know the sufferings that are about to befall you. I ask you to listen, to listen to Me! I am truly Jesus Christ and I come to you this day and I beg you to spend your waking hours spreading My love throughout this world! I beg you to help save souls from damnation. Your actions are so important to Me and the plan of the Father. You are here because you are called and you have answered this call. Each and every one of you present I send into this world as warriors to spread My love. You listen and you take it so lightly but you will know that I am truly calling you for this world is in such sin and pain. To the little work that you do I will apply My grace to lead souls to My Most Sacred Heart. Surrender and become one in Me for I truly am calling you to the highest union for it is in this union that I can operate through you. As long as you resist My call there are many souls that will not be touched. I beg you to take Me seriously. Meditate on this statue (the Pieta). Meditate on this, My children.

9. **Jesus:** I carried My cross on My back And I fell under the cross. See Me as I crawl with the cross on My back.

10. **Jesus:** This is the love that I have for each and every soul. The bodily agonies I experienced were nothing compared to the agonies I experienced in My Heart for the souls that would be condemned to eternal damnation despite My sufferings. I beg you this day to answer My call.

Song between decades: I come to you with greatest love...

Jesus Is Crucified and Dies on the Cross

1. **R.** He hung for three agonizing hours against the darkened sky. He gave His flesh! He gave His blood! He gave the last beat of His Heart, the last breath in His body! Covered with blood and weakened, He hung on the cross!

2. **Jesus:** I speak and so many do not listen! I am crying out to you to listen to My voice here, to read My letters for they are truly letters of love that I give to each one of you. It is in reading these letters that you will know more and more the immensity of the love that I have for you. You are My soldiers that I send into the sick world with the medicine to heal so many hearts. You are the chosen ones I have called here to this Center. Please, I beg you, take My call seriously, for I am truly Jesus

and I speak to you this day. So many take My plea lightly. I beg!
I plead! I ask Rita to talk more and more about My pleadings.
You do not know how I am longing for you to be so close. How
I want you to surrender and let Me operate in your hearts! You
tap ever so lightly when there is an ocean of My love that I want
to give to you. Surrender your hearts and read My letters of
love for it is in these letters that you will know My love more
and more.

3. **Jesus:** I give Myself to you at every Eucharist and you take it so
   lightly! Take Me seriously, My children, for I am truly with you
   with much love! How it wounds My aching Heart that you do
   not listen.

4. **Jesus:** I am sending you into battle in a world that is godless,
   that has forgotten God, but with your hearts filled with My love.
   Will you answer My call?

5. **Jesus:** Surrender! Surrender! Surrender to the God Who gave
   His life for you!

6. **Jesus:** As Mary walked by My side on the way to Calvary, as
   she stood under the cross, she is by your side in all your sufferings. You are never alone.

7. **Jesus:** I give you My very own Mother!

8. **R.** As she held His little baby body, she now holds His lifeless
   body in her arms under the cross.

9. *Song:* At the cross her station keeping stood the mournful
   Mother weeping. Close to Jesus to the last.

10. **R.** This rosary is from the Hearts of Jesus anad Mary, so united,
    one with each other. To love Jesus is to love Mary. To love
    Mary is to love Jesus.

Song after last decade: I come to you with greatest love…

ROSARY MEDITATIONS
MARCH 30, 1995
THE JOYFUL MYSTERIES

Mary appeared in the Sorrowful Mother Chapel for two hours.
The whole corner was adorned in the most brilliant celestial light
with a pink hew. Marty and I will never forget the experience of

this evening. Jesus illuminated in the Sacred Heart statue during the litany and the promises of the Sacred Heart. Jesus requested that this rosary be circulated to all.

The Annunciation

1. **R.** The Angel Gabriel appeared to Mary and asked Mary to be the Mother of Jesus.

2. **R.** Mary always complied with the Will of the Father. Jesus always complied with the Will of the Father. In looking at their lives we see how they always lived according to the Father's Will. It is in living according to His Will that our true joy and happiness lie.

3. **R.** She was filled with the Holy Spirit and the Word became flesh and dwelt among us.

4. **R.** Picture the Virgin Mary as vividly as you possibly can and see Mary as she carries the child Jesus within her womb.

5. **R.** She conceived the child Jesus. Mary, a spotless virgin, conceived Jesus, the Son of God. He was inside of her! She was bursting with the life that was God's life radiating from her very being!

6. **R.** Do we realize how God wants to be one with us? The more we become united to Him, the more His presence radiates from within us and shines to those that we come in contact with. God is so good that He sent to this world His only begotten Son through the Virgin Mary. He sent His Son because He loves us and He yearns and longs and thirsts for us to be ever closer to Him. It is in His presence within us that we will light up this world. It is in our oneness with Him that we will shine as little lights to the rest of the world.

7. *Song:* O holy dwelling place of God. O holy temple of the Word. O holy Mary, holy Mother of God!

8. **R.** God so loved the world that He sent His only begotten Son into this world, incarnate in the womb of the Virgin Mary. The Word became flesh! God took on flesh!

9. **R.** As Mary contained the presence of the Almighty God, as He grew within her womb, His Sacred Heart was formed in her womb through the power of the Holy Spirit. He remains with us this day in the sanctuary of the tabernacle. His same presence is there. God, in His divinity and humanity, truly present in the tabernacle, longing for us to come and to share our lives and

our time with Him.

10. **R.** I see before me so clearly the Virgin Mary as she carried the child within her womb. It seems beautiful to think of Mary carrying the child Jesus within her, but the risen Lord is with us this very day! He remains with us in greatest love but His Heart is wounded by the indifference and the neglect of His chosen souls, the ones He loves so dearly, that totally neglect Him and treat Him so coldly.

Who are we that God is so good that He sent into this world His only begotten Son and that He loves us so much that He created us in His own image and likeness? We are His creatures but He raises us to such heights in His divine life.

Song between decades: Come, Holy Spirit, fill our hearts. Enkindle in us the fire of Your love. Come, Holy Spirit, fill our hearts. Enkindle in us the fire of Your love.

The Visitation

1. **R.** Mary made haste to the hill country to visit her cousin Elizabeth who also was with child.
2. **R.** When she arrived, the child in Elizabeth's womb leapt for joy.
3. **R.** And Elizabeth cried out in a loud voice, "Of all women you are the most blessed and blessed is the fruit of your womb! Why should I be honoured with a visit from the mother of my Lord?" (Lk 1:42,43)
4. **R.** And the child in her womb leapt for joy!
5. **R.** Mary cried out in a loud voice the Magnificat!
6. *Song:* My soul rejoices in God, my Savior. My spirit finds its joy in God, the living God.
7. **R.** For He Who is mighty hath done great things to me and holy is His name!
8. **R.** John the Baptist, even in his mother's womb, leapt for joy. Prepare ye a way for the Lord! He is truly coming and He is in our midst this day. Jesus Christ, the Son of God, is truly present and we stand around and balk and do not realize the immensity of the great gift that He has given us. Fill our hearts with Your grace so that we may be gifted with courage to go out and spread the Good News, the news of His great love to all the souls that He longs to be close to. For truly, if we love Him, it is our duty to go out and tell others of the immense love He has

for them!

9. **Jesus:** I call out to you this day, My beloved ones, for I am truly present. You are My chosen ones that I call upon to unite ever so closely to My Heart. I send you into this world among the wolves that will bite at you and grab at you. You must be strong soldiers to spread My love throughout the world. Will you not answer this call for I am calling with such an ardent plea? Please, I am begging you to take this plea seriously.

10. **R.** Prepare ye a way for the Lord for He is truly coming! He is in our midst this day. Go into the highways and the byways and spread the Good News for you truly possess the keys to the Kingdom of Heaven!

    Jesus: Let your hearts not be heavy but light, filled with the fire of My love. Ascend upward and upward. Do not be dragged down by the perils and the sins of this world for I am filling you with My divine life and My divine love. You must forever ascend upward, always with your eyes cast upward toward heaven for you are My soldiers that I send into this world to spread the Good News to all those that are hurting and in pain. I call out to you. Do not worry for what is happening around you.

Song between decades: Come Holy Spirit, fill our hearts…

The Birth of Jesus

1. **R.** The child Jesus was born in the town of Bethlehem in such poverty. He was born in a stable because there was not room for Him in the inn.

2. **R.** See a little, tiny baby, so helpless! A baby that cannot do anything! God, in all of His might and power, came to this earth as a little, tiny baby!

3. **R.** His way always was to comply with the Will of the Father. Mary always lived according to His Will. It is in complying to the Father's Will that we will know true peace and joy in our lives.

4. **Mary:** I am the Immaculate Conception. I am here with you, my beloved ones. I call out to you to pray fervently, for the days ahead are days filled with suffering. This world has lost its way. You must pray fervently for all beloved souls. I call you to pray this rosary every day. Pray the rosary as you have never prayed from your heart before. Be filled with the love of my Heart and my Son, Jesus. Be forever wrapped in our lives.

Come, come to the Hearts of Jesus and Mary and be led deeply into our immense love for you. Pray, my little ones, for sufferings are to come, deep sufferings. This world is disobedient. They will not obey the laws and commands of my Son. I have come! I have called! I am ignored! My dear ones, my sweet ones, I tell you, I tell you to pray. Listen with your ears open and your hearts filled with the love of God. It will be your strength for the dark days that are ahead. I am the Immaculate Heart. I call out to you, my beloved. This rosary is a tool that will draw many hearts to the Hearts of me and my Son.

5. **Mary:** I pray with you, my little ones. Each prayer that you pray should be connected with me and my Son and the angels and saints and the souls in purgatory. You are praying as one with the courts of heaven. Lift high your hearts! Lift your voices and join with us!

6. **Mary:** I pray for this world, for this world that is sinful and godless. I ask you to pray fervently and to come to my Most Immaculate Heart.

7. **Mary:** How my little children suffer, little children that are so young! Men's hearts are so cruel and filled with self. I beg you to go out and spread the love of my Son to this world. You must stayed fixed on Him!

8. **Mary:** My Heart bleeds and I cry bloody tears for the slaughter that is happening to the young ones. As my child was a baby in my arms, I call out to you to pray fervently for the little ones, for they are being persecuted far beyond anyone's comprehension from the ways of this world. My precious little children!

9. **Mary:** I am the Mother of all!

10. **Mary:** I am the Immaculate Conception and I am truly present and with you. Men will not listen. They will not turn from their ways. You must pray as you never prayed before. The times at hand are times of great suffering. I am calling out to you to spread this message to the world, for this world is not listening. Who is here to pray with you? Three! Three of you are here and I am in your midst! Men do not care for their world. They hold on to their world and I tell you over and over again to pray the rosary. I am truly present and I am here with you!

Song between decades: Come, Holy Spirit, fill our hearts...

Mary: I am the Virgin Mary and I wish for you to pray in this room tomorrow night.

The Presentation of Our Lord in the Temple

1. **R.** Mary and Joseph went to the temple with the Child Jesus in their arms. Simeon, the prophet, was there and told Joseph and Mary of the sufferings that Jesus and Mary would have to undergo.

2. **Mary:** My Heart was pierced with a sword so many times through my Child's life. My dear ones, people will suffer because they will not listen. They are willful in their ways. I call out to you to spread these messages in any way that you can, for I am truly speaking to you here and times are so short. My dear ones, carry this message out to this world, for sufferings are at hand!

3. **Mary:** I call you to come on the fifth of April and pray the rosary here in this room.

4. **Mary:** Bring with you all that will pray, for sufferings are at hand. You will suffer such immense sufferings. You need to pray! Pray the rosary! Tell all to come and be with me in this room to pray the rosary!

5. **Mary:** I have held back the hand of my Son! He will call upon the earth and there will be such suffering, my beloved ones. You tarry too long! These messages of His love must circulate! You do not know what is about to befall the earth. I call out to you this day to listen to me for, as you see me illuminated before you, you know that what I speak to you is true.

6. **Mary:** Pray! Pray! Pray!

7. **Mary:** I am Our Lady of Light and I appear to you to take this message to this world this day! Carry this message to every person and tell them what I tell you here!

8. **Mary:** My Heart was pierced with a sword as I stood beneath the cross of my Son! As He gave His life, His flesh and His blood for love of you, my Son loves each and every soul. He died for them! I beg you to go into this world and to spread His love to every corner of this world. You can not hold back! Souls will be lost because they did not know the love of my Son. You are in a position, for He is speaking to you, to carry this message to those who are hurting. Feed the hungry souls with the love of my Son!

9. **Mary:** Let your hearts be filled with my light! May you have

the courage that the Holy Spirit will give to you so strongly to transform you from fear to fearlessness, to carry out the plan of the Father. You are my lights to shine to this darkened world! Let your hearts be opened and go, my children! Go! I summon you to go and to not hold back!

10. *Song:* I come to you with greatest love, I am your loving Savior. I am your God, I died for you. I come to you this day.

Mary: I will make myself known to those who come and pray this rosary!

Song between decades: Come, Holy Spirit, fill our hearts...

The Finding of Jesus in the Temple

1. **Mary:** I would like my Son Jesus present in the tabernacle when you pray this rosary!

2. **Mary:** My Son was taken to the Temple for the feast of the Passover. We lost my Son in the Temple. So many souls this day are in deep darkness and have lost their way. They are dead in their hearts! I pray to you to go out to this world and spread the good news! You are so favored by God that you are given such great gifts! To hold them to yourself is not to His liking! I beg you to spread this news, to pray for courage, to do what He is asking you to do!

3. **Mary:** He has chosen this Center to be apostles to go out into the world and to spread the love of His Most Sacred Heart through my Most Immaculate Heart. Can you not answer the call that I give to you this day? You are so favored, so chosen, so gifted by God Himself and you bicker and you fight and you complain! You, my chosen ones, the chosen race, look at you!

4. **Mary:** You look at each other with eyes of envy when God is speaking here! Each person that receives this message is receiving a grace, a gift from God Himself! You do not even see! You are so blind!

5. **Mary:** Pride is an evil that ruins men's hearts. Speak to all men of pride. It is only a loving heart that will unite with the Heart of my Son. A heart of love will light up this darkened world. I send you as soldiers into a world that is godless! You are fighting a battle with this world, with hearts full of the love of my Son. Look at all the souls that are lost! Look at the children of these parents who have gone astray! Little children! Look at their

lives! I am so sad for the lives of my children. I call to you this day. Look at your world, America! You are so blind! You do not see! You have turned deaf and you have closed your eyes! I come and I appear! My Son talks and so many do not pay Him heed! I beg you! I beg you to heed my words for I truly am Mary, and I am speaking to you!

6. **Mary:** Hearts that are hard, hearts that are godless, hearts that are lifeless, hearts that are dead in sin! Look at your world, America! Can you turn your head and look the other way? I come and I plead with you to turn your hearts back to the love of my Son, and who listens? Three come to pray my rosary with me! How do I shake those into listening to me here for I am truly speaking in this rosary to my beloved children? Listen to me! All those who come to this rosary will receive abundant graces from me and my Son!

7. **Mary:** My lost children, how the fires in hell burn, burn so brightly for the souls that were willful and had their own way. You do not see! You do not comprehend! You focus on little details here in your lives! Focus on the fires of hell, my dear, sweet children. Souls are burning in the fires of hell for their own willfulness and sin, and many more will be lost despite the sufferings of my Son. Many souls will be lost. I call you to unite with the Heart of my Son, to go into this world and preach the Gospel at every highway and byway, to spread the love of my Son, Jesus.

8. **Mary:** My little, lost children, I am your Mother, and I lead you on your way, closer and closer to Heaven!

9. *Song:* O holy dwelling place of God. O holy temple of the Word. O holy Mary, holy Mother of God!

10. **Mary:** Tomorrow is the 31st of March and I tell you to come to this chapel and pray the rosary in this chapel at 6:20 p.m.
    Song after the last decade: Come, Holy Spirit, fill our hearts...

ROSARY MEDITATIONS
APRIL 16, 1995
THE GLORIOUS MYSTERIES

This rosary was delivered on Easter Sunday in the Sorrowful Mother Chapel. Jesus came alive in the large Sacred Heart picture. He came out of the picture. Marty saw clusters of angels around the Sorrowful Mother statue. Mary and Jesus moved their eyes.

The Resurrection

1. **Jesus:** It is in your suffering that you will have immense union with Me.

2. **Jesus:** As I died and rose on the third day, you, in your suffering, will rise to new life in Me.

3. **Jesus:** You have come to Me and I am here waiting for you to share this time alone with you. Put your minds at rest and unite ever so closely to My Most Sacred Heart.

4. **R.** Death has no power over Jesus! On the third day He rose victorious from the tomb, His body glistening in white. He truly rose to bring us new life. We are partakers in His divine life. The gift that we receive is far beyond our comprehension.

5. **Jesus:** You are as the Easter lily. You come from a narrow place and you grow more and more in this life with Me. You will bud and blossom forth and My life will radiate to this world as you become absorbed and saturated with the divine life that I impart to you.

6. **Jesus:** My power is endless for I am truly here and present in this room with you. Feel the vibrancy of My presence with you. I am Jesus Christ, the Son of the Living God, the resurrected Lord. I live and am present with you this very day.

7. **Jesus:** The world has closed off their hearts. They have come, their hearts are hardened, their faces are hard. I am life! You must go out to this world and give the message of My immense love. Tell this world that I am alive and I have risen, that I am in your midst this day, that I live in such an abundant fashion in the hearts of men who are in the state of grace. You, My children, are so blind! I am so present to you! God lives and is in

your midst and you do not see. You run down useless roads and look for such foolish things. Oh, how I love you, My beloved. I call you to a state of urgency to spread My message to this world.

8. **Jesus:** As you are in your hearts, so shall you be in this world. I am Jesus, the risen Lord. I live on in the hearts of men this day. What you do here will affect the lives of so many souls. I beg you to preach the Gospel, to pray for fearlessness to carry this message to the hearts of all men.

9. **Jesus:** I am totally with you in this room. You do not realize the immense gifts that I give to you.

10. **Jesus:** In Body, Blood, Soul and Divinity, I am present! The risen Lord is with you, My beloved souls, this very day!

Song between decades: Come, Holy Spirit, fill our hearts. Enkindle in us the fire of Your love. Come Holy Spirit, fill our hearts. Enkindle in us the fire of Your love.

The Ascension

1. **Jesus:** Before I ascended into heaven, I gave to the apostles the power to baptize and forgive sins. I give to My beloved priests this day this power through the Church. I give to each priest the power to change bread and wine into My most precious Body and Blood. How I love My Church and love My beloved priests-sons, for they are truly called. I live in this world today through My anointed ones.

2. **R.** See Jesus as He raises His arms and ascends into heaven and a cloud takes Him from our sight. We live on faith. We see the consecrated Host but we do not comprehend the great gift we have that He truly remains with us this day in the consecrated Host. God gives Himself to us! We become one in Him when we receive Him in the Eucharist. He gives us His Body.

3. **Jesus:** Do you see these mysteries, how glorious they truly are that I died and rose on the third day and then ascended into heaven?

4. **Jesus:** I am Jesus Christ, the Son of God, come to this earth in such great love to save souls, to lead souls to heaven to be with Me forever and ever. How many souls will be lost because of their willfulness and their ways? Pray, My children, for the souls that are in darkness. They hold on to their foolish ways. They turn their backs and go their own way.

5. **R.** He went to heaven to prepare a place for us. Heaven is our true home!

6. **R.** He ascended into heaven and the gates of heaven were opened!

7. **Jesus:** I send you as missionaries into this world to spread the Gospel of the Lord Jesus Christ.

8. **Jesus:** You say: "For You, Lord, anything! For You, Lord, I will do anything!" And I call you to speak out in front of people and you say, "I can't do that, Lord!" I call you to pray to the Spirit for the courage to preach the Gospel for there are many who are suffering and in pain. Hear their words: "You helped me get to heaven"!

9. **R.** See the souls as they ascend into Heaven behind Jesus. See the souls as they are released from purgatory because of our prayers. See the great mercy of God that He loves souls. God the Father loves us so much that He sent His Son into this world so that we might be in heaven some day.

10. **Jesus:** See the souls of those living this day, and see them, as they die, being condemned to eternal damnation for their willfulness. For sin is sin and I came to give you life!

Song between decades: Come, Holy Spirit, fill our hearts...

The Descent of the Holy Spirit on the Apostles

1. **R.** Jesus promised before He left the earth that He would send the Holy Spirit to baptize the apostles. Please, dear Holy Spirit, descend upon us so that we have the courage to do all that You are asking us to do. We are fearful and weak and we need Your grace. We need You to live in us, to operate in us, to help us be more and more like Jesus.

2. **R.** Who is our model? Whom do we model ourselves after?

3. **R.** Mary was joined in the Upper Room with the apostles and a gigantic wind came and there appeared over their heads parted tongues of fire.

4. **R.** They were filled with the Holy Spirit and transformed from fear to fearlessness. They went out to preach the Gospel and all understood!

5. **R.** Holy Spirit, descend upon us! Outpour all of your gifts and please give to us the courage to be able to carry out the mission that the Father has intended for us.

6. **R.** Where we are, as humans, weak and afraid, saturate us with

the fire of God's love so that as we operate, we operate enlightened by You. We receive Your wisdom, Your understanding and Your knowledge to know exactly what the Father is calling us to do.

7. **R.** Mary, our Mother, help us to unite ever closer to the Holy Spirit that He can work and be active in our being, that we might feel this saturation and penetration of the presence of the Almighty God within our souls.

8. **R.** Holy Spirit, impart to us Your life so that we may be enlightened to do all that God is asking us to do. Fill us with such a brilliant light that we know the light of the Almighty God.

9. **Jesus:** I am the Way, I am the Truth, I am the Life! He who abides in Me will have the light of life!

10. **R.** May we be transformed more and more into the image of Jesus in the Heart of the Virgin Mary and led to the bosom of our Father.

Song between decades: Come, Holy Spirit, fill our hearts...

The Assumption of Mary Into Heaven

1. **Jesus:** Model yourselves after Mary, My Mother. She was taken body and soul into heaven as you, too, some day will be taken into My kingdom.

2. **Jesus:** You must come to our Hearts. Pray from the heart, My beloved ones. As Mary was so united to My Heart, pray to Mary to unite yourselves closer and closer to My Heart.

3. **Jesus:** The more you live this rosary in your daily lives, the more you will pray from your heart. It is in understanding Our lives that you will be joined closer to Us.

4. **Jesus:** Our Hearts are a great symbol of Our love for you.

5. **Jesus:** How is your heart? Is your heart free of all debris to unite with My immense love? Purify your hearts and come ever closer to Me for a heart that is full of sin cannot unite with My Heart. My Heart is pure and filled with love. To unite closely with Me, your hearts must be forever pure.

6. **Jesus:** How I want to unite with each one of you in deepest love, to unite more deeply with you. The love that I have is immeasurable and the longings of your hearts are the longings to unite ever closer to My Heart. You will be satisfied in heaven, My beloved ones, for your hearts will be filled with My love.

7. **R.** Mary went to heaven and united closely with the Father, the

Son and the Holy Spirit in a most intense union.

8. **Jesus:** Your hearts crave this love that only I can give. Search you this barren desert and you will never satisfy the cravings in your hearts.

9. **R.** Mary mothers us as she mothered Jesus. Mary is the Mother of the Church. We pray to Mary to lead us to an ever deeper union with God.

10. **R.** We pray to Mary to lead this Church into deeper union with Her Son, to help the priests and the religious who are our ministers in this Church, to lead the souls to deep and longing love with Jesus Christ, the Son of God.

Song between decades: Come, Holy Spirit, fill our hearts...

Mary Is Crowned Queen of Heaven and Earth

1. **R.** Mary reigns with her Son in the courts of heaven! The Sacred Heart of Jesus will reign on this earth! The Immaculate Heart of Mary will triumph! There will be an era of peace, but many will suffer the loss of their souls for their own willfulness.
   Jesus: You are a big part of the Father's plan to help souls to know of the love of God. I beg you to pray fervently from the heart and to lead others to the love of My Heart.

2. **R.** How the Heart of Mary knows the Heart of Jesus. How she stands by our side and mothers with the most maternal love. How do we turn to Mary? Do we realize that she is here at every second waiting to take us to the Heart of her Son? She reigns in heaven with her Son Jesus. He loves His Mother so much. Ought we not put our faith and trust and love in His Mother so that she might lead us closer to His Sacred Heart?

3. **R.** We are the children of God. God is our Father. Let us realize how we must live in connection with the Father, that our every action is to please Him and to do His Will, that Mary is our Mother and by our side with love to lead us to greatest union with God.

4. **Jesus:** Do you want peace, joy and happiness, or do you want your own wills? Only in submitting to the Will of My Father will you have peace, joy and happiness.

5. **R.** Mary is there to lead us to the Heart of her Son.

6. **R.** The Heart of Jesus is waiting to be united with us in such deep love. Help us, Jesus, as little children being held by our loving mother, to realize the immense love that the Father, the

Son and the Holy Spirit outpour to us. Help us to realize how Mary is our Mother who guards us and protects us under her mantle, how she watches over us and leads us ever closer to the Heart of her Son.

7. **Jesus:** The glory is in the resurrection! The glory is in the new life! I lead you into glory but you must submit your wills to the Will of the Father.

8. **Jesus:** This intense union that I want with each one of you far surpasses anything you could find on this earth. Come to Me and sit with Me in front of My tabernacle. Be joined in oneness as I give you My very Body and Blood as your food to eat. I nourish you with My own Flesh and Blood. I become one with you and you become one with Me. As we are united, you become united to the Father, for I am one with the Father and He is one with Me. My beloved ones, the great gifts that I give to you and you are so blind!

9. **Jesus:** Consecrate your lives to the Sacred Heart of Jesus and the Immaculate Heart of Mary and pray fervently for your priests, for I live this day in the Church. Pray for the priests and the Church. I love you, My beloved ones, and I love My Church.

10. **Jesus:** Feed the hungry! My love is enough! People do not realize the immensity of My love. They scratch only the surface and I have such deep love to give. If you focus always on My love, you will be fed. You will know struggles and trials, but in all of these struggles, you will be brought to deeper life with Me. As you experience thorns, I give to you a bed of roses. I am Jesus, My beloved ones, and I have spoken directly to you of those things that I hold in My Heart and wish to share with you. Open up your hearts and your souls and ponder the words that I have spoken here. I truly long to be closely united to you, My precious chosen ones. Pray, pray, pray! Men have turned their backs. They have walked away and in their willfulness, they have forgotten God. I come to bring you new life that you might have it to the full.

Song: I am the Bread of Life. He who comes to Me shall not hunger and who believes in Me shall not thirst. No one can come to Me unless the Father beckons. And I will raise you up.

And I will raise you up. And I will raise you up on the last day.

Jesus: Pray for My beloved priests and for the Church, My dear ones. Pray for the courage to go out into this world and be a witness of the love of God that you have within your hearts. It is fear that stops you from spreading this message. You, too, will be joined with Me forever and ever in heaven. I ask you to go out into the world and tell all you meet of My great love for them.

Locution Received After
Recitation of the Seven Sorrows

Jesus: I stand at the door of the hearts of mankind and knock. Many close their hearts and walk away. My beloved ones, pray for the souls of your brothers that they will open their hearts and let Me enter. Your prayers are so important for the salvation of many souls. Pray, My beloved ones! Pray as you have never prayed before. Unite ever more closely to My Most Sacred Heart. Pray always in union with Me and My Mother, the angels and saints, and the souls in purgatory. Pray to the Father, in union with the Holy Sacrifice of the Mass, in the Spirit. Your prayers are so valuable to many souls. Do not underestimate the power of prayer. I call out to you this day to go as soldiers into this world.

— During Easter Sunday (April 16, 1995) Rosary
Our Lady of the Holy Spirit Center, Norwood, Ohio

ROSARY MEDITATIONS
FOR PARENTS AND CHILDREN
APRIL 20, 1995
THE JOYFUL MYSTERIES

The Annunciation

1. **R.** The Angel Gabriel appeared to Mary and asked her to be the Mother of God.
2. **R.** I see all through Mary's and Jesus' lives how they complied with the Will of the Father.
3. **R.** The Father has a plan. Jesus was incarnate in the womb of

the Virgin Mary. Jesus came to this earth in quietness. This was part of the Father's plan. Mary always complied with the Father's Will. When she said, "...let it happen to me as you have said" (Lk 1:38), she was showing her willingness to do whatever the Father was asking her to do.

4. **R.** Jesus came to this earth to show us the way, to teach us the way to get to Heaven.

5. **R.** Each beautiful soul is a creation of the Father. How He loves each person He creates!

6. **R.** The Father loves us so much that He sent His only Son into this world as a sacrifice, to pay for the sins of mankind.

7. **R.** Mary was a virgin and she said to the angel: "But how can this come about...?" (Lk 1:34) And the Holy Spirit came upon her and she conceived the Child Jesus through the power of the Holy Spirit.

8. **Mary:** How I love little children to pray My rosary. Teach your children about the lives of Jesus and Mary.

9. **Mary:** Pray the rosary with your children.

10. **Mary:** It is in living as a little child of the Father that you will be the happiest, that you will go to heaven some day.

Song between decades: Ave, ave, ave Maria. Ave, ave, ave Maria.

Mary Visits Her Cousin Elizabeth

1. **Mary:** Jesus said, "Let the little children come to Me." Teach your children how to pray. Teach them when they are young. Your children need to know about God.

2. **Mary:** Children are so precious to Jesus! My dear little ones, teach your children to pray the rosary.

3. **R.** Mary went with haste to visit her cousin Elizabeth, who had conceived a child in her old age.

4. **R.** The child in Elizabeth's womb was John, who would prepare the way for the coming of Jesus.

5. **R.** When Mary arrived at Elizabeth's house, with Jesus in her womb, the babe in Elizabeth's womb leapt for joy.

6. **Mary:** I call out to the children of this world to come and pray. Prepare ye the way, for my Son is truly coming and you will know the immensity of His love. My children, you will be the leaders of this world!

7. **Mary:** Model your families after the Holy Family.

8. **Mary:** What a price my Son paid for your salvation. He came

to show you the way.

9. **Mary:** Jesus is truly present in the Eucharist, the same as when I carried Him in my womb, the same as the day He walked on the earth! Should you not jump for joy as the babe in Elizabeth's womb jumped?

10. **Mary:** My dear little children, I am Mary, your Mother. How dearly I press you to my Heart. I am forever with you!

Song between decades: Ave, ave, ave Maria. Ave, ave, ave Maria.

Jesus Is Born in Bethlehem

1. **Mary:** My dear little children, my Son was born in a stable in the town of Bethlehem in such poverty. He was God and He came to this earth in such poverty for greatest love of you! Can you not turn your minds and hearts to Jesus? Jesus truly died for love of you. My dear little children, you are missing the greatest treasure of all. Jesus loves you so much!

2. **Mary:** How your Father cares for you! He created you so specially, with such special gifts. My little children, turn to Jesus, my Son. He came to this earth a helpless baby. This, the Son of God!

3. **Mary:** Jesus wants you to come and make your home in His Heart.

4. **Mary:** Jesus loves you so much. His Heart is on fire for you, His precious little children.

5. **Mary:** How this world has turned away from God! My dear little children, God created you. God loves you!

6. **Mary:** He is in your world this day. My dear little children, how can this world deny God? He is in your every breath, in your every heartbeat. You are dependent on Him for your life!

7. **Mary:** In such simplicity my Son was born in the town of Bethlehem. The animals were there to give Him warmth.

8. **Mary:** This is God's world and you are chosen as His special children. You are part of His plan. You must stay rooted in God.

9. **Mary:** My Son was born in the town of Bethlehem and the stars shone brightly above where He lay. My little children, the Almighty God was born a helpless baby for love of you.

10. Hail Mary...

Song between decades: Ave, ave, ave Maria. Ave, ave, ave Maria.

The Presentation of Jesus in the Temple

1. **Mary:** Your hearts were made for God. You will not be happy, my dear little children, if you turn away from Him. It is only in turning your hearts to God that you will know true love and happiness.

2. **Mary:** We took my Son to the Temple, and Simeon the prophet told me of the sufferings of my Son. He died on the cross so that you would get to heaven. My dear little children, I am your Mother. I guard and protect you. Jesus gave His life so you would be with Him forever and ever.

3. **Mary:** He knocks on the door of your heart and only you can let Him in.

4. **Mary:** I knew from the prophecy of Simeon how my Son Jesus would suffer. My Heart was in such sorrow to know of the sufferings to come!

5. **Mary:** But, my dear little children, how my Heart is in such deep sorrow to see the children of this world and watch them suffer. Little innocent ones murdered as babies! Little children taught about sex in schools! My precious children, pray for your world, for your prayers as children are so powerful. How Jesus loves children to pray!

6. **Mary:** This rosary is for my beloved children of this world. It is sent to you from my Immaculate Heart. My beloved children, will you answer your Mother's call to come and pray the rosary with me every day? Pray with one another, for your earth will suffer for its sinfulness and willful ways. I am calling you, children of America, to unite and pray. Pray the rosary every day.

7. **Mary:** My beloved children, pray to the Child Jesus. He will answer your prayers.

8. **Mary:** My Heart was pierced with a sword. His Heart was pierced with a lance. Sufferings will befall this earth! Children of America, unite and pray!

9. **Mary:** Know how my Son loves you, that He gave His life for love of you.

10. **Mary:** What a great gift you received when you were baptized, for you were given a share in His divine life. My beautiful children, how I love you!

Song between decades: Ave, ave, ave Maria. Ave, ave, ave Maria.

Mary and Joseph Find Jesus in the Temple

1. **R.** The Child Jesus, when He was twelve years old, was taken to Jerusalem to celebrate the feast of Passover.

2. **R.** When the Passover celebration was over, Joseph and Mary left with the caravan and the Child Jesus was left behind.

3. **R.** When they realized that Jesus had been left behind, they went back to Jerusalem, their hearts in such sorrow in search of the Child Jesus.

4. **R.** Jesus was talking to the doctors in the Temple.

5. **Mary:** Jesus wants to fill your hearts and your souls with His life. The Holy Spirit wants to release in you the gift of His wisdom. Open up your hearts, my beloved children. Pray to the Spirit to lead you into closer union with my Son. Pray to the Child Jesus!

6. **Mary:** Jesus lived on this earth as a little child. He lived as you live on this earth. This was God, the Son of Man! Out of greatest love for you, my little children, my Son came and lived on this earth.

7. **Mary:** Think, my little children, how close you are to your mother. Stay close to me. Stay rooted in my Immaculate Heart. Know that I am forever by your side, guarding and protecting you. I place my mantle securely around your shoulders. Do you feel the protection that I give you? You are children living in a troubled world. How you are wounded by the sin in this world! I am your Mother and I will protect you. You must turn to me. You must pray to me. Pray the rosary, my children. This is your weapon against Satan, for the world is evil. Satan wants to trip you up, my children. Children, listen to your heavenly Mother, for I love you with the deepest love.

8. **Mary:** This rosary I have given especially to you, my children. Pray this rosary with your friends for it truly comes from my tender Heart to your heart.

9. **Mary:** If you ever wander from Jesus, turn to me! As I searched for the Child Jesus, know that I am here and I will lead you back to the Heart of my Son.

10. **Mary:** My dear little children, pray to me and to the child Jesus for your friends that are lost. I truly love each and every precious one of my little children. Turn your lives to my Son, Jesus. He waits and longs for you. He loves you. When this world is

cold, turn to the child Jesus.

Song after the last decade: Ave, ave, ave Maria. Ave, ave, ave Maria.

Mary: This is a rosary from my Most Immaculate Heart for my beloved children. I ask you to circulate this rosary to my dear children, for they are being taught lies in this world. If they are being taught lies, is it not your duty to teach them the truth? If you have received this rosary, I ask you to spread it to the children. For my little children are my dear, dear little ones. They need to pray. Children are not praying. Please, I beg you. Spread this rosary to all little children for I love them so much. How powerful are the prayers of little children! I am Mary, your Mother. Thank you for responding to my call.

ROSARY MEDITATIONS
FOR PARENTS AND CHILDREN
APRIL 21, 1995
THE SORROWFUL MYSTERIES

The Agony in the Garden

1. **Jesus:** Agony of agonies! How I suffered, My dear ones, in the Garden. I saw before Me all the sins of all men from all time. I knew the souls that would be condemned to eternal damnation despite My suffering.

2. **Jesus:** People do not want to hear this day. They plug up their ears and close their eyes. Children are being murdered in their mother's wombs!

3. **Jesus:** I saw before Me all the vileness in men's hearts, the cruelty they do to one another. How My Heart was wounded, for I love souls so dearly.

4. **Jesus:** You were created by the Father. You are His precious creation.

5. **Jesus:** How He loves the little children of this world! They are so precious to Him!

6. **Jesus:** I saw before Me all the suffering I was about to experience.

7. **Jesus:** I asked My Father that, if it were possible, this cup be

removed from Me, but, not My Will, but His Will be done.

8. **Jesus:** My apostles–those that I loved–they slept!

9. **Jesus:** My little ones, can you not come and pray with Me? I asked My apostles to spend one hour with Me and they slept! Those that I loved and wanted to be close to slept!

10. **Jesus:** I am your best friend Jesus. I gave My life for you that you could be with Me in heaven. My little ones, how I love you and want to be so close to you.

Song between decades: I come to you with greatest love, I am your loving Savior. I am your God, I died for you. I come to you this day.

Jesus Is Scourged at the Pillar

1. **R.** Jesus was led away. They pulled His hair! They poked Him and hit Him! They took Him away and tied Him to a pillar!

2. **R.** What did Jesus do that these men felt they could put Him to death?

3. **R.** How hard it is sometimes to walk in this world today, to stand up for God when others have forgotten Him.

4. **R.** They took Jesus, tied Him to a pillar and whipped Him with harsh instruments that tore His skin and made Him bleed.

5. **R.** This is your best friend, Jesus. He is God! He came to earth so that we might be with Him forever in heaven. See Him covered with wounds, deep wounds, His marks of love covering His entire body!

6. **Mary:** Tell your children to pray the rosary. I am Mary, your mother. I give to you this rosary to spread to the children of this world. It is the rosary that will draw their hearts closer to my Son, Jesus.

7. **Mary:** They untied my Son and led Him away, covered with wounds, whipped and beaten.

8. **Mary:** Your friends may persecute you, my little children. They are cruel sometimes. Know that Jesus is your best friend. He loves you so much that He suffered the scourging at the pillar.

9. **R.** Do you know how it is to love someone and have them treat you cruelly. Jesus loves each and every soul so much that He suffered and died for them. How He is treated cruelly by those souls He loves so dearly!

10. **R.** He asks you to love all men! There is not one soul that He would not give His life for. He asks you to love those that are

cruel to you, to be kind to all men, to follow in His ways. His ways are always gentle. His ways are kind. His way is the way of love.

Song between decades: I come to you with greatest love…

Jesus Is Crowned with a Crown of Thorns

1. **Jesus:** They took Me and gave Me a throne. They covered My bloodied wounds with a dirty robe and then pounded sharp thorns into My head.

2. **Jesus:** They laughed—a cruel, hateful laugh! They laughed and spit in My face and called Me a king! These were the souls that I gave My life for.

3. **Jesus:** You will be persecuted for My sake. The world has turned away from God. They have made other things their gods. They want themselves to be supreme. My children, pray for your world, for your prayers so please the Heavenly Father.

4. **Jesus:** Your friends are cruel to you. Love those who are cruel! People that are cruel are hurting inside.

5. **Jesus:** You must forgive. Pray for grace from the Spirit to transform you to be more like Jesus.

6. **Jesus:** Mary walked by My side all through My life. She is your mother. She walks by your side. Every minute of the day, your mother is with you.

7. **Jesus:** You are My little saints in this world. I love you so dearly and want to be so close to you. I never leave you. I am your beloved Jesus, Savior of the world.

8. **Jesus:** You will suffer from those who you wish would love you. But look how I suffered, My little ones! See Me as they spit in My face and hit Me on the head. The blood ran from My mouth from the blows they gave to My head. This is the love that I have for you.

9. **Jesus:** Do always the Will of the Father. He loves you, My dear, little children. Listen in your heart and you will hear Him speak to you.

10. **Jesus:** Children need to pray to the Holy Spirit. Ask the Holy Spirit to be your friend, to be with you and to guide you on your way.

Song between decades: I come to you with greatest love…

Jesus Carries His Cross Up Calvary

1. **R.** Jesus carried a heavy cross laden with the sins of the world.

2. **R.** He did not give up His cross. He carried His cross. He did not complain. Covered with wounds and covered with blood, He carried the cross on His back.

3. **Jesus:** I ask you to carry the little crosses I give you this day. It is in carrying these crosses that you will grow closer to Me.

4. **Jesus:** Satan wants you to be willful. He wants you to demand your own way. The way to Me, to the Father, to heaven, is to do the Will of the Father.

5. **R.** Covered with blood, He could scarcely go on. He fell under the cross three times. He did not give the cross up. He collapsed from the weight of it.

6. **R.** How closely united Jesus is to His mother. His mother was with Him in such close union His whole life. Now their eyes meet on the way to Calvary. In that meeting of the eyes there is such joy to see each other but such sorrow to watch each other suffer.

7. **Jesus:** My dear, little ones, I call out to you and ask you to pray for your friends in school.

8. **Jesus:** When you see people who are mean, pray for them. They are hurting in their hearts.

9. **R.** The Father, Son and Holy Spirit live inside of you every minute when you are in the state of grace. They live in such a special way within your very heart.

10. **R.** Make your hearts pure and model your lives after the lives of Jesus and Mary.

Song between decades: I come to you with greatest love...

Jesus Dies on the Cross

1. **R.** The greatest of all agonies, the agony of the Heart! How Jesus loves each and every special child!

2. **R.** He loves them so much that He gave His flesh and blood for each and every soul.

3. **Jesus:** The Father, out of greatest love, gave you a free will. I died on the cross. It was My Father's Will. But I remained at peace for I knew the Father's love. The Father loves you, My beloved children. Go to Him, talk to Him. Know that He loves you deeply.

4. **R.** Jesus has not gone. As He gave His life on the cross, He

gives His life this day. He is here in His humanity and His divinity in the consecrated host, longing and waiting for you to come and be alone with Him.

5. **R.** We want God to be more like us, but God is as He is. God is a mystery! Give us the grace to know more and more the mystery of God.

6. **R.** When we are persecuted, help us to see before our eyes the crucified Jesus, to know that He was persecuted.

7. **R.** Mary is calling you to holiness. Will you turn your hearts to God?

8. **R.** Souls that are holy are at peace.

9. **R.** When you have love, you have joy!

10. **R.** The way to God is to love.

Song after the last decade: I come to you with greatest love…

ROSARY MEDITATIONS FOR PARENTS AND CHILDREN APRIL 26, 1995 THE GLORIOUS MYSTERIES

The Resurrection of Jesus

1. **R.** Jesus died and, as had been foretold, He rose on the third day. Death has no power over Jesus!

2. **R.** They had rolled a gigantic stone up to the tomb where Jesus had been buried. The stone was rolled away. Mary Magdalene and some of the other women came to put spices on Jesus.

3. **R.** There were two men and they said to the women at the tomb, "Why look among the dead for someone who is alive?" (Lk 24:5)

4. **R.** Mary was weeping and she saw a man she thought was the gardener and it was Jesus.

5. **R.** Jesus appeared to His beloved apostles and they did not recognize Him at first.

6. **R.** The apostles did not understand all that Jesus had told them.

7. **R.** We must pray to God to open up our minds and hearts so that we may understand Him more, for He is a mystery!

8. **R.** He gave to the apostles the power to baptize and to forgive

sins. It is through Baptism that we are reborn into new life.

9. **Jesus:** My dear little children, you are chosen by Me to be My special, anointed ones. In Baptism, you were made children of God and heirs of heaven.

10. **Jesus:** My dear little children, how dearly I press each one of you close to My Heart.

Song between decades: Come, Holy Spirit, fill our hearts. Enkindle in us the fire of Your love. Come, Holy Spirit, fill our hearts. Enkindle in us the fire of Your love.

The Ascension of Jesus into Heaven

1. **R.** See Jesus as He extends His arms and goes up to heaven. See the apostles below. They are filled with fear and confusion to see their beloved Jesus leave.

2. **R.** These are the Glorious Mysteries. Our hearts are filled with such immense joy to see Jesus rise from the dead and go up into the sky! Think of this!

3. **R.** God is a mystery! We can meditate on this mystery of Jesus rising from the dead, of His going up to heaven. He wants us to meditate on the mysteries of His life and His mother's life.

4. **R.** He wants us to live His life, death and resurrection in our lives this day.

5. **R.** God the Father loved us so much that He created us in His own image and likeness. It is in meditating on the mysteries of Jesus' and Mary's lives that we can model the way we live after Jesus and Mary.

6. **R.** Jesus gives us a special calling at baptism to go out and show others His immense love, to tell others about our good God Whom we love so much.

7. **R.** Jesus has not left. He remains with us, truly present, the same as the day He walked the earth. He remains in the Eucharist in His divinity and His humanity .

8. **Jesus:** My dear little ones, how I love you. When you are baptized, the Father, the Son and the Holy Spirit dwell inside of your Heart in a very, very special way. I am Jesus. I never leave you. I love you and remain with you in your heart.

9. **Jesus:** How I love my dear, little children. Bring the children to Me! Bring the children and sit in front of the tabernacle. Tell them that I am Jesus and how I love them.

10. **Jesus:** I wait for you, My little children, to come and tell Me

that you love Me, too. I wait for you to come and to talk to Me, to share all those things that are in your heart with Me.

Song between decades: Come, Holy Spirit, fill our hearts...

The Descent of the Holy Spirit on the Apostles and Mary

1. **Jesus:** I sent to the apostles the Holy Spirit to dwell within them. The Holy Spirit transforms you, My little children. so that you are not afraid. Pray to the Holy Spirit. Ask Him to help you to have the courage to talk about God in front of your friends.

2. **Jesus:** As you love your mother, your father and your friends, I love you and Mary loves you so much more than any earthly person could ever love you.

3. **Jesus:** The Father created each one of you so specially! He loves you so much!

4. **Jesus:** He gives you the special talents that you have this day. He loves you so much and wants you to use your talents to do the work of God.

5. **Jesus:** The Holy Spirit is such a dear friend! Pray to the Holy Spirit every day for He loves you so much.

6. **Jesus:** The Holy Spirit lifts your spirits. Satan is in this world and wants to keep you depressed. Pray to the Holy Spirit to lift your hearts high and to be filled with God's love.

7. **Jesus:** Let the little children come to Me! Bring them to Church and pray with your children. My dear, little children, pray the rosary.

8. **R.** Think about the stories of the lives of Jesus and Mary. Think about how Jesus died on the cross for love of you.

9. *Song:* Come Holy Ghost, Creator blest, and in our hearts take up Thy rest. Come with Thy grace and heavenly aid, to fill the hearts which Thou hast made, to fill the hearts which Thou hast made.

10. **R.** Holy Spirit, set our hearts on fire with the fire of God's love!

Song between decades: Come Holy Spirit, fill our hearts...

Mary Is Taken Up Into Heaven, Body and Soul

1. **R.** Mary is our beloved mother. She loves us so much! Jesus gave to us His very own mother!

2. **R.** She loves us far more than any earthly mother could ever love us.

3. **R.** Her love is a personal love.

4. **R.** The more we realize how close our mother really is to us, the more we will feel secure as she wraps her mantle about us and leads us ever closer to her beloved son, Jesus.

5. **Mary:** I wrap you, my beloved, dear, sweet children, in my arms. I hold you close to my Heart. I protect you from this world as any mother would protect her little child. You are my little child, my dear one. I am forever with you.

6. *Song:* Immaculate Mary, your praises we sing. You reign now in splendor with Jesus, our King. Ave, ave, ave, Maria. Ave, ave, Maria.

7. **R.** Jesus, when He ascended into Heaven, went to prepare a place for us. The gates of heaven were opened!

8. **R.** Now Mary, some twenty years after Jesus' death, was taken into heaven. But Jesus and Mary are here with us this day! Jesus dwells within us and remains in the tabernacle, truly present.

9. **R.** We, too, will be taken up into heaven. These are the Glorious Mysteries. If we love and serve the Lord, we will be given such glory in Heaven.

10. **R.** My dear, little ones, let the lives of Jesus and Mary grow in your hearts. Meditate on these mysteries and learn more about their lives. Always pray to the Spirit to lead you into deep meditation.

Song between decades: Come, Holy Spirit, fill our hearts…

Mary Is Crowned Queen of Heaven

1. **R.** The Immaculate Heart of Mary will triumph! The Sacred Heart of Jesus will reign! There will be an era of peace!

2. **Mary:** My beloved ones, you will have a period of struggle. Stay close to the Hearts of Jesus and Mary.

3. **Mary:** Our Hearts are a symbol of greatest love for you.

4. **Mary:** In your wildest imagination, you cannot image the deep and most tender love that my Son has for you. Pray to the Spirit to open your heart so you may feel more and more the great love that Jesus, my Son, has for you.

5. **Mary:** God wants you to be joined with Him forever and ever in the courts of heaven. You must, every minute of your life, seek after holiness. The devil goes about this earth prowling and aiming to trip men in their paths. My dear, little ones, Jesus, my Son, loves you with the deepest love. Focus on the love of Jesus.

6. **Mary:** I call to you! I call to you! I call to you! I am Mary, the

mother of God, and I am your mother. My dear little ones, harken to my call, for you are my chosen ones.

7. **Mary:** You are commissioned through baptism to go out into this world and spread the Gospel of the Lord Jesus Christ. Do not hold back but let your hearts be forever open and the love of God will flow from you and radiate from your very being.

8. **Mary:** I am Mary, your mother! My beloved children, how I love you with the most maternal love. I love you! I love you! I am waiting for you to come closer to my Heart.

9. **R.** Help us to be more aware of the great gifts that you are giving to us this very day. Help us to be sensitive to the grace of the Lord, our God.

10. *Song:* Hail Holy Queen, enthroned above, O Maria. Hail Mother of Mercy and of Love, O Maria. Triumph all ye cherubim. Sing with us ye seraphim. Heaven and earth resound the hymn: Salve, salve, salve, Regina!

Song after last decade: Come Holy Spirit, fill our hearts…

ROSARY MEDITATIONS AT A SHEPHERDS OF CHRIST MEETING JULY 11, 1995 THE SORROWFUL MYSTERIES

The Agony in the Garden

1. **Jesus:** My dear ones, Satan is pressing hard on many of My beloved souls. Sufferings are about to befall this earth. You must hold tight to My Heart for he aims to stop you. You are My beloved soldiers that I am sending into this world to carry forth My love. Hold tight, My dear ones. I am giving you abundant graces for all the trials you are facing daily. I am attentive to your every need, minute by minute, second by second. I am guarding and watching you. You must come to My Heart through the Heart of My beloved Mother. Nestle ever so close to the Heart of My Mother, My dear ones. Come into her loving arms and let her caress you and lead you gently into My Heart, burning for love of you.

   I am Jesus. Do not fear. Do not feel pressed on by Satan.

Come to Me and meditate on My passion. It is in realizing My intense love for you that you will have peace and joy in your life and know My constant presence with you. I am Jesus, I am with you. I am depending on you to go into this world and be strong soldiers. Hold tight to My hand, My beloved ones. Focus on My love for you.

2. **Jesus:** When you think that nothing else can go wrong, My dear ones, and something else goes wrong, you are being tried. For the days ahead will be dark and hard. Realize that these are gifts that are helping you to grow in holiness and in virtue.

3. **Jesus:** I mold you into special gems, My dear ones, My beloved ones, My precious ones. I long for your love.

   I long for a heart that is set so deeply in love of Me! Will you answer My call to unite? Be a heart that is burning with deep love for God. You are so precious to Me! A heart filled with love is so dear to Me and comforts My aching Heart!

   My dear ones, so many of My beloved ones treat Me with such indifference and ingratitude. How My Heart is warmed by your burning love. Will you come to Me? Will you join in deepest love with My burning Heart, on fire for love of you.

4. **Jesus:** Know that, as you go each day, as you suffer all through the day with different trials, different obstacles that are put in your path, I am with you as you struggle. See Me as I knelt in the garden. I suffered so for the ingratitude of all of the souls that I loved with deepest love, souls who would reject Me. Many times you are faced with rejection by those that you love. My dear ones, when you are faced with sufferings and crosses, come to Me. Meditate on My life. Focus on the sufferings in My life and how they parallel your life. You will grow more deeply in your life with Me.

5. **R.** Jesus knelt in the garden and, in His divine knowing, He knew all of the souls from all time, all of their sin, all of the vileness in the hearts of men. He also knew all of the acts of love, the burning love of His precious souls who come and spend time with Him. This love was sweetness during His bitter passion.

6. **Jesus:** Many in the world this day are blind and do not see. My dear ones, because you do not see with your earthly eyes, do not think that I am far. I am with you, ever by your side, guarding

and protecting you. The Father is watching you. Your Mother is by your side. Let the Spirit live within your being and operate you as you go about your lives. Know the presence of the Almighty God, the Father, the Son and the Holy Spirit, within you. Go inside of yourself and feel the presence of God, the Father, the Son and the Holy Spirit.

7. **Jesus:** You will be pressed on by Satan, through much mental torment and anguish, and people that you love, those closest to you that seem to hurt you. I am allowing this, My dear ones, so that you may be strengthened for the days ahead. You are My soldiers. I am testing you. I am sending you out as shining stars in the darkest night. I am Jesus. I love you with the deepest love. Come to My Heart and I will bathe you in a bath of My precious love.

8. **Jesus:** The heart and its ways! Many have closed their hearts and turned cold. They operate with a gaze that is hard and focused. Open wide your hearts. Let your hearts be soft and supple.

   Let your heart be the light of your body and the life of your soul. I am filling your heart with My life. Be open and remove all of the blockages to your heart. Let me penetrate your heart and fill you with vibrant divine love. I am Jesus. You are My light that will shine in the darkest night.

9. **Jesus:** My dear ones, I want you to meditate on My sufferings. This will strengthen you in your sufferings. In all your sufferings, stay rooted in Me. You will experience deeper and deeper life in Me. Your days are a constant suffering and rising to new life. Accept all that is given to you and focus on Me. Every moment I want to be so close to you! I want your thought to be focused on Me every moment of your day, a constant awareness of the presence of God. You will have peace and joy in your hearts even in times of struggle. I am Jesus, your beloved Savior. I came to this earth to save you from your sins.

10. **Jesus:** My Mother nurses you with the milk of salvation. Let go and be bathed in the love of Our Two Hearts. As I suffered in the Garden, I was comforted by your acts of love this day. Comfort My aching Heart, come and outpour your love, for I am waiting and longing and thirsting to hear the words of your love from your lips. Will you come, My beloved? I am the

bridegroom of your soul, waiting for your precious soul to unite with Me. Will you come? Will you unite for our wedding? I am Jesus Christ and I am waiting for you.

The Scourging at the Pillar

1. **R.** It is through the Body and Blood of Jesus that we are saved. Think of the price He paid for our salvation.

2. **R.** I see Jesus tied to the pillar, His body unmarred. Then they begin to beat Him with such harsh instruments! They tear His flesh and wound His beautiful body. When I think of the little irritations that I allow to bother me each day, I see Jesus with His body covered with wounds.

3. **Jesus:** It is in your struggles that you will find comfort when you meditate on My passion and the stations of the cross. My dear ones, I am giving you abundant grace when you meditate on My passion, the stations of the cross and the Sorrowful Mysteries. It is there you will find much comfort from the struggles you are experiencing. Come to My Heart and let Me bathe you in unending love.

4. **Jesus:** The starved soul searches and wanders for love. I am present to you in a special way, My dear ones, outpouring My love to you. Do you feel the love that I am giving to you at this moment? Stop. Make a Spiritual Communion. Feel the presence of the Almighty God within your heart. Release and let go of all of the anxieties of the day, all of the distractions that have occurred with your family and friends. Focus totally on My love for you and My presence within.

5. **R.** I see before me the gigantic wounds on the arms of Jesus, My Savior. The wounds are open wide, exposing the interior of His body. I know the little crosses that I am asked to carry that seem so monumental. They seem so minute when compared to His wounds!

6. **R.** It is in meditating on the relationship between Jesus and His Mother that I experience much warmth in my heart.

7. **R.** If we were really there and saw the men as they beat our beloved Jesus, would we believe then the immensity of His love? It is through His life, His suffering and His death that we are saved from our sins. Blessed Jesus, I place my trust in You.

8. **R.** How hard it is many times to trust and surrender when we are backed against a wall and the sufferings seem so monumental.

It is in meditating on these Sorrowful Mysteries that our hearts are softened and we realize the immense love that Jesus has for each one of us. He gave His Flesh and Blood for each and every soul. He died for each person and He asks us to love God and our neighbor, to love those that are kind and those that are not so kind, to love all our brothers.

9. **Jesus:** Let your hearts be soft and supple. Come to Me, My beloved ones, and I will bathe you in My Heart filled with love. Let go of all hatred, anger and resentment and look at your brothers through My eyes. I suffered, I was scourged, for your beloved brother. My dear ones, will you not love him for Me this day? Many of your brothers are hurting and in pain and you will carry out My love to this hurting world. Surrender and let go of all resentments, of hatred and anger. It is hard, many times, to follow My way. I am giving you abundant graces. I am showering you with My love. You know the Heart of Jesus. Can you not share this Heart with all you meet? Lift your hearts to God. Pray to the Spirit to be lifted high and filled with vibrancy.

10. **R.** His back was scourged and He walked away from the pillar covered with wounds, but His Heart was filled with love and His eyes were gentle and loving, for He loved each and every soul unconditionally and He proceeded on His way. As He was crowned with thorns and carried His cross to His death on the cross, He loved each and every soul.

The Crowning with Thorns

1. **R.** His head was crowned with a crown of piercing thorns. They pounded the thorns into His head. The thorns tore His flesh.

2. **R.** He stood. They spit on Him. They mocked Him. They called Him a King. Jesus Christ, the King of all Kings, whose Heart is filled with burning love, such gentleness! To each one of us He says, "I love you, I love you, I love you," His Heart filled with love for His persecutors!

    Jesus: My dear ones, think of the little crosses you are asked to carry this day. Think of how they treated Me, and I am God! You will suffer and you will receive much persecution for My sake. My dear ones, pray for the grace to be strong. Satan aims to stop you. I am giving to you abundant graces to withstand all of your sufferings. I love you, I love you, I love you. You are My beloved ones. I am Jesus. I give Myself to you. Come to the

Eucharist. I will give you Myself.

3. **Jesus:** Little thorns on your way! Little thorns that lead you to greater life in Me! Little ones, I know you are struggling this day.

4. **R.** If Jesus sat and was crowned with thorns, if they spit on Him and mocked Him, can we not stand the vile words of our brothers? Words wound us sometimes, words from those closest to us. Satan knows how to get to each one of us. He works on those that are closest to us. Dear Jesus, give me the grace to love more and more as You loved.

5. *Song:* Give me Your Heart, O Jesus, give me a heart like Yours. Teach me to love You with this new heart. Oh, I know little of how to love You. Create in me, oh, precious Savior, this special heart.

   Jesus: I allow you to suffer many sufferings for you are being strengthened.

6. *Song:* Crown Him with many crowns, the lamb upon His throne. His regal scepter knows no bounds, all kingdoms are His own. All Christians come and sing, to Him who died for thee, and hail Him as thy Savior King for all eternity.

7. **R.** So precious, the head to the body, and they gave to Jesus a crown of thorns.

8. **Jesus:** Can you not love your brothers this day? See My face, covered with blood, and My head crowned with thorns. This is the love I have for you. Will you not love your brothers that are in this world, those hurting and in pain? I am Jesus. I am sending you into the world as My special apostles of love.

9. **Jesus:** Pray as you have never prayed before, for prayers can stop wars. Pray the rosary and meditate deeply on the mysteries of Our lives.

10. **R.** Touch me, Jesus, with your burning love.
    Song: Little baby hands and feet…

The Carrying of the Cross

1. **Jesus:** I carried My cross up Calvary and the road became harder and harder. I fell under My cross. My face hit the earth. My dear ones, you carry crosses that get heavier and heavier. Look at me as I carried mine and look at Me with My face on the ground. This is the love that I have for you. Do not give up in all your trials and struggles. You are My beloved ones. You

must come to My Heart. Let Me fill you with My strength. You cannot give up. Meditate on this mystery as I went on and on and on and it became harder and harder as the cross became heavier and heavier.

2. **Jesus:** Satan wants you stopped. You must pray for grace to have joy in your heart, for you are given great gifts and I am giving you the messages of My love.

3. **Jesus:** The night may be dark and cold but in your heart the light of My love shines brightly.

4. **Jesus:** The First Commandment commands that you love God with your whole heart, your whole soul and your whole being. It is through your example that the others will see the love in your heart. My dear ones, do not go backwards. Come to Me and let Me fill you with such vibrancy. You will go into this world and show all a heart that is filled with the love of God.

5. **R.** Veronica wiped His blood-covered face.

6. **Jesus:** I know your every thought far better than you yourself, My dear ones. I know what is in your hearts. I am so attentive to all of your needs, all your struggles, all your pain. Do you believe Me? I am Jesus. You do not know the tender love I have for you. I am here and I am pouring out to you tender love.

7. **R.** His eyes met the eyes of His beloved Mother. Her face was reddened and covered with tears. His eyes and His face were covered with blood. As their eyes met there was such intimacy between the Son and His Mother. They had known that this day would come. In that look they shared their grief and their love.

8. **R.** He fell a second and third time and He was forced to get up, always in compliance with the Father's Will. To His death on the cross He gave His all for love of us.

9. **Jesus:** The sun may not shine, the stars may cease to shine, but, My dear ones, you will have My light within your heart. Your hearts will be filled and lighted with this love. As you walk in darkness you will feel an interior warmth in your heart. You will know the presence of Father, Son and Holy Spirit. If you are in the state of grace, We dwell within your heart in such a special way.

10. **Jesus:** No matter what your cross is, know that you are never alone. Focus on this presence within you, the presence of the Almighty God. Know the love of your Father. Think of this: a

Father that loves you with the deepest love and is dwelling within your heart.

The Crucifixion

1. **Jesus:** Sufferings may befall the earth but you will not fear for you will feel the presence of the Almighty God within you. At this moment feel this presence so close to you.

2. **Jesus:** Come to My Heart. Take refuge from the scorching sun in My Heart. I hung for three agonizing hours on the cross. You, too, will remain in peace, for you will know the interior presence of the Almighty God within you.

3. **Jesus:** Feel the warmth within you and surrender, My dear ones. When you are backed up against a wall, surrender. Take all of your cares and put them in the arms of the Almighty God. I spread My arms on the cross and gave My all for love of you. Do you think I am not listening to your prayers this day? I am Jesus. If I gave My life for you, do you think I would abandon you now? I am so attentive to all of your needs.

4. **Jesus:** Come to Me, My little child. I feel your heart so filled with fear. I am gentle and kind of Heart. I give you My abundant love. My Mother nurses you with her milk. You are so loved by the Hearts of Jesus and Mary. Surrender. Do not be in fear. I do not want you to fear, My precious little child. Come as a baby at the breast and surrender to your loving Mother and your loving Father.

5. **R.** Such love Jesus had for each one of us that He gave the last beat of His Heart! He could have at any time stopped what was happening. He had complied with the Will of the Father for love of us. Then He gave the last beat of His Heart.

6. **Jesus:** Come to Me, My beloved ones. My Mother nurses you with the milk of salvation. I am Jesus. I love you, I love you, I love you. Mary stood beneath the cross. I gave you, My beloved ones, My very own Mother to care for you.

7. **Jesus:** Mary is caring for you as she cared for Me, forming you forever in her Heart, through the Holy Spirit, to be more and more like Me. My dear ones, you were created in the image and likeness of God. Surrender and let Us work in you.

8. **Jesus:** You are being polished and purified. I want hearts that are filled with love. I am the bridegroom of your soul. I gave My life for love of you. Will you come and give your heart to Me?

9. **R.** I consecrate my heart to the Hearts of Jesus and Mary. His Heart was pierced with a lance. Her Heart was pierced with a sword.

10. **R.** It is through His pierced Heart that the sacramental life of the Church was formed: water, a symbol for baptism; blood, a symbol of the Eucharist. We are given His divine life in baptism. We are fed through His very own Body and Blood. Mary is the Mediatrix of all graces and His life flows through her Heart. It is through Mary's Heart that we are dispensed this life, merited by Her Son as He gave His life on the cross.

July 11, 1995 Shepherds of Christ Meeting

Mary: My dear little children, I am Mary, your Mother. I have called each one of you here to hear my plea. This world is hurting and in pain. My little children suffer so. Will you be my little children that go out and spread the love of my Son Jesus to the world? It is in your actions that many are taught the lessons of His love. I speak to you gently for I love you with a gentle Heart. My Son Jesus loves you with a Heart of deepest love. Surrender and let go and let Our love penetrate your heart and fill you. I am protecting you with my motherly mantle. I am holding you in my arms and pressing you close to my Heart. I am giving to you my motherly love. Surrender and feel me as I hold you in my arms and give you the milk of salvation. I am Mary your mother and I am forever with you. My precious, precious little children, pray for all my little children on this earth.

ROSARY MEDITATIONS
BEFORE EXPOSED BLESSED SACRAMENT
IN THE HOLY SPIRIT CHAPEL
OUR LADY OF THE HOLY SPIRIT CENTER
JULY 13, 1995 NOON
THE JOYFUL MYSTERIES

The Annunciation

1. **R.** Put yourself in the presence of the Almighty God. Before us is the same Jesus Christ who walked on the face of this earth

and was carried in the womb of the Virgin Mary. He is present, the same Jesus who hung on the cross. Who are we that the Almighty God is present and that we are before Him? Let us bow our head and bend low for this truly is Jesus Christ, the Son of God, and He is giving to us a great gift by allowing us to be so close.

2. **R.** We see the angel appearing to the Virgin Mary and asking Mary to be the Mother of God. Mary says yes to the angel, always complying with the Will of the Father. She loved the Father so much as a little child, always wanting to please the Father.

3. **R.** Mary is filled with the Holy Spirit, and the Word became flesh and dwelt among us. Jesus, the Son of God, enters this earth in the womb of the Virgin Mary. Who are we that God the Father so loved this world that He sent His only-begotten Son, Jesus into this world? Jesus took on a human baby body.

4. **R.** We are His chosen ones. The Father created us with such love, each one of us individually, so precious to Him. He gave to us His Son that we would be saved and live with Him forever and ever in heaven.

5. **R.** To help the mysteries of the rosary live in our life, we must meditate on the intimacy between Jesus and Mary. We see the Two Hearts, The Heart of Jesus and the Heart of Mary, beat within the body of Mary. In two of the mysteries of the rosary, Jesus is inside of Mary's body. There is such intimacy between those Two Hearts. In two mysteries of the rosary, the Hearts are enclosed in one body, beating together in the body of Mary.

6. **R.** Realizing this intimacy between Jesus and Mary can help us come closer to God. Mary is the key to intimacy with God.

7. **Jesus:** Let your hearts be soft and supple, My dear ones. Open wide your hearts and rid yourselves of all distractions of this world. Be alone with Me. I am Jesus Christ, the Son of God, and I am giving to you great gifts here, abundant graces to under-stand more the mysteries of My life and that of My Mother. Open wide your heart and forget all that is holding you apart from Me and meditate on these mysteries of Our lives.

8. **Jesus:** Make a Spiritual Communion. Feel the presence of the Almighty God as you do when you receive Holy Communion. For when you are in the state of grace, the Father, Son and Holy

Spirit dwell within you in such a special way! You cannot imagine the beauty of a graced soul, a soul that is filled with My life. If I lifted the veil in this room, you would fall on your faces from the vibrancy of the rays that would come from the Consecrated Host. My dear ones, you do not know the great gifts I am giving to you in this room.

9. **R.** Always in compliance with the Will of the Father, Mary said yes to the angel and the Son of God was conceived within her womb. Mary mothers us this day and dispenses to us the life that was merited by Her Son on the cross. As Jesus was formed in the womb of His Mother through the Holy Spirit, we too are formed in the spiritual womb of our Mother. She dispenses life, the life of grace, to us as we are transformed more and more through the Holy Spirit into the image and likeness of Jesus, her Son. Who are we that God loves us so much?

10. **R.** As you meditate on these mysteries of the rosary, see the connectedness between the Hearts of Jesus and Mary. Mary's Heart that dwells in Her Son. Let your heart dwell in the Heart of the Virgin Mary and your heart will dwell in Jesus' Heart. You will be in such connection with this love, the love of your Mother and the love of Jesus, your Savior.

The Visitation

1. **R.** The Virgin Mary goes to visit Her cousin Elizabeth. The child in the womb of Elizabeth leaps for joy at the presence of the Almighty God. Here we are in this room and the Almighty God is present, no less present than He was in the womb of the Virgin Mary. The child in Elizabeth's womb leaps for such joy! Let our hearts be filled with joy that God is here and has chosen us to be with Him. Nothing is an accident. Every hair of our head is numbered.

   He calls and we respond to this calling. He is by our side, with us every second, as we go about our day. He is so attentive to each and every one of our needs! He is talking in our hearts in such a gentle and kind voice, outpouring His gentle words of love. We do not hear many times, in the busyness of our lives. We do not hear the sweet and gentle words that He speaks in our hearts. So gently He tells of His love for us and of His longing to be ever closer to us. We put Him aside and go to the world. Our hearts are aching and begging for love. He says over and over again, "Come to Me. I am what your soul seeks and I am waiting. When your hearts are breaking and in pain, you must come to Me." It is then that you will be comforted and you will receive the desires of your soul. Nothing on the face of the earth can fill the starved soul but the love of the almighty God.

2. **Jesus:** Many are called, but few are chosen. My dear ones, I have chosen you and My Mother has called you to this house. You are My apostles that will go into this world, laden with pain and suffering, and spread the love of God. This is not a little task. I am applying My grace to your lives. You will be fearless as you go about this world doing the work I am calling you to.

3. **R.** Mary goes to Her cousin Elizabeth, one person with whom to share the good news. We see in the windows in this chapel, across from the Visitation window, the Assumption into heaven, and then her Coronation as queen of heaven and earth. Her life and the life of Jesus unfold as They comply always with the Will of the Father. Always living in peace and joy. They knew the Father had a plan and They wanted to please Their beloved Father. We do not see that, from the day we were born, the Father had a plan for each one of us uniquely created with a mission far beyond our own comprehension. We seek for such little things, when the Almighty God is calling and leading us on our way. We are so precious to the Father! Dear Holy Spirit, open up our eyes and our hearts. Help us to realize the greatness which He has bestowed on us. Help us to realize that the Almighty God–Father, Son and Holy Spirit–dwells within us. If we could see the state of our own soul, a soul in the state of grace, we would not believe the beauty of this soul.

4. **R.** It is in baptism that we are made children of God and heirs of heaven. We are children of God! God loved the world so much that He sent His only Son, so that we would be with Him forever in heaven. This is only a stopover on our way to eternity. The glory that awaits us is so immense that we can never comprehend it.

5. **R.** Mary visited Her cousin Elizabeth with the child Jesus within Her womb. We are visited by Jesus in this room in such a special way! For the Almighty God is outpouring His abundant grace to each one of us at this time. Mary, help us to be more sensitive to the touch of His Grace, to realize His life, the vibrancy of this life, within us.

6. **Jesus:** Many are called, but few are chosen. I have chosen you, and My Mother has called each one of you to Her house. This moment, moment by moment, second by second, you are being guarded and watched in this world that is suffering and in pain. You do not see the great gifts that I am outpouring to you. Open wide your heart. Let go any bitterness, anger and resentment, and live according to the Father's Will. Operate in love. Do all your deeds in love, and know that your Father is guarding you. Your Mother is forever by your side protecting you. Father, Son, and Holy Spirit dwell within your heart in such intimacy. My dear ones, children of God, open your hearts and receive the graces that I am giving to you now.

7. **Jesus:** Prepare ye a way for the Lord. John the Baptist prepared a way for the Lord. I am sending you this day as My apostles into this world. Many will know My ways from the love in your heart. You are My apostles. It is through your example that you will teach many. The lessons to be taught are the lessons of love. You will be judged on how you loved God and loved one another. Like ripples on a pond, one act of love is transmitted and many hearts are touched. My dear ones, open wide your heart and let Me penetrate your soul with My abundant life.

8. **R.** Mary went to visit Her cousin Elizabeth with the good news. We see the outcome. We see Mary in the windows in this church. The apostles are beneath her. The Holy Spirit descends upon them. They are filled with the Holy Spirit and go into the world. We see their efforts in the world today. We do not see the greatness that occurs when we plant the seeds.

9. **Jesus:** Let not your hearts be troubled. Satan is pressing down and dividing many of My beloved ones. You must focus on My Heart and know that Satan is at work here. When you are harboring ill thoughts toward any person, Satan is attempting to divide you. Let your hearts be free and your minds be open. Pray for grace to deal with all of the sufferings that you are undergoing. It is in My grace that you will be strengthened. Pray every day for abundant grace to know and love God more. Come to the Eucharist and sit before Me in front of the Tabernacle. I give you My life. You will go about your duties. You will be free in your heart for it is My power that will power you. I am the Almighty God. You are My soldiers that I am

sending into this world. In this world, You go into battle every day. I am guarding you and watching you, loving you and protecting you and filling you with My life.

10. **Jesus:** Come to Me, My beloved ones. I want to hold you close to My Heart. I want to caress and cuddle you and give you My love. I am Jesus, your Savior. I love you. I love you. I love you.

The Birth of the Lord Jesus

1. **R.** The Hearts of Jesus and Mary beat within the same body. Is there more intimacy than that? For two mysteries of the rosary we see these Two Hearts joined in one body. In the third mystery, the child Jesus is born. Mary was the life support of the physical life of Christ. Although Their bodies are now separated, the life of the child Jesus continues through the milk of His Mother.

2. **R.** Jesus gave to us His Mother who stood beneath the cross. He gives to us a share in His divine life, merited by His life and, in a special way, by His death on the cross. It is through Mary that we receive this life. She is the Mediatrix of all grace. She gave Jesus the life of his physical body. Grace flows through her to us. It is through Mary that we will be drawn closer and closer to the Heart of Jesus.

3. **R.** The sheep and the shepherds are around the child Jesus. Jesus Christ, born in a stable, in a manger, in the town of Bethlehem. The Chief Shepherd of the flock, a little baby, comes to this earth. He is not born high and mighty, with gold and silver. Rather, He is wrapped in swaddling clothes and laid in a manger, surrounded by sheep and beasts of the earth.

4. **R.** In the windows in this church we see the child Jesus in His manger, raised above His sheep. We see, in the window across from Jesus' birth, that He is raised above the apostles and going into heaven. Jesus comes to feed His lambs and His sheep. He remains with us in the consecrated Host, but He leaves behind His Blessed Mother and the apostles to carry out the work that He began.

5. **R.** It is through the apostles that this Church is spread throughout this world. He calls us to be His apostles this day, to go into the world and spread this love. He is Chief Shepherd of the flock. He sends us to feed the hungry souls with His love. Jesus gives us His life in the sacrament of baptism. He nourishes this

life by His Body and Blood in the sacrament of the Holy
Eucharist.

6. **R.** He no longer walks this earth, but He remains, in His divinity and humanity, no less present today than the day He did walk the earth. He remains in the consecrated Host. He is as present in this room as the day He was born in the town of Bethlehem. Who are we that we have the Presence of the Almighty God? Where Jesus is, so are the Father and the Holy Spirit, for They are three in one. He is so closely united to Mary, His Mother. Mary is also present with us.

    Jesus: Many are called, but few are chosen. I have chosen you this day, and I am showering you with My abundant grace, the grace of My life.

7. *Song:* Come unto Me…

8. **Jesus:** I give to you. I am the Almighty God. I have all the power. What have you to fear when I have chosen you and you have responded to My call? The Father is pleased with your efforts, My dear children. Live always to do the Will of the Father and you will live in peace and joy.

9. **Jesus:** I have not come to this earth to divide, but to save men from their sins. I came to this earth to love all of My beloved ones, more and more. My dear one, release all of the anxiety and fear in your heart. Let Me bathe you in a bath of My love. I am Jesus and I am truly present and attentive to all your needs.

10. **Jesus:** This love is poured into your heart and you know more and more the presence of the Almighty God. Feel this presence within you. Release and let go of all distractions. I am the Almighty God and I am truly present.

The Presentation of Our Lord in the Temple

1. **R.** The child Jesus was taken to the Temple and presented to the Father.

2. **R.** Mary was told by Simeon of the sufferings to come. He said to Mary, "…and a sword will pierce your soul too." (Lk 2:35)

3. **R.** Jesus, in His divine knowing, knew at all times all that would occur. Although He was a little baby that could not talk, He was the Almighty God and He knew of all the sufferings. Mary, His beloved Mother was told by Simeon of the sufferings to come. We see in many of the pictures, like the one of Our Lady of Perpetual Help, the looks on the faces of Jesus and Mary, for

they shared within Their Hearts the deep secret that they knew that the cross would come. They went through Their lives and shared this secret in Their Hearts of the sufferings to come. They knew that Jesus would suffer. Simeon said to Mary, "…and a sword will pierce your soul too." (Lk 2:35) A sword pierced the Heart of Jesus, and what came forth was blood and water, the birth of the sacramental life of the Church. This life flows through the pierced Heart of the Virgin Mary, for she is the Mediatrix of all graces. It is through her motherhood that we receive the life of Christ. As Christ received His life within Her womb, so we receive His life in the Church through the Virgin Mary. We receive this life through our Mother.

4. **R.** Let our hearts be filled with the life of the Almighty God. May our hearts sing, for we are given great gifts. In this room today, the Almighty God is present. His Mother is with us, mothering us and loving us.

5. **R.** Who are we that we are called to this Center, and that Jesus and Mary speak to us? This is a mission to spread the love of the Almighty God to the world. We must be attentive to this call, for God is calling us to do this work. We must let God work in our lives. We must silence the prompting of Satan to divide us. We must silence all of the negative thoughts within our minds and recognize that they are coming from Satan. We must pray for the grace to realize the great gifts that we are given. The Almighty God has chosen us. Many are called, but few are chosen.

Jesus: I have chosen each one of you. If you are hearing this message, you know you are hearing it because the Almighty God is calling you to a special mission. You are My soldiers that I am sending into the world to spread My light to all the dark corners. I am giving you great graces to do the work at hand. Open wide your hearts. Let go of all anger and resentment, any thoughts you have against your brothers, and love them. I call you to love, to love all men. I shed My blood for them. Love and you will be free. If you hold on to anger and resentment, your heart will be troubled and at unrest.

6. **Jesus:** Satan aims to trip you up and stop you in your path. The Almighty God is speaking to you. What have you to fear? Father, Son and Holy Spirit live within your heart. If the world

shakes and the sun ceases to shine, within your heart you can feel the presence of your Father, Son and Holy Spirit so close to you and loving you. Release all your anxieties and let Me bathe you in a bath of My love. I am Jesus, and I am outpouring to you My life.

7. **Jesus:** The seeds of time move exceedingly slowly, but I see all time as one. My dear ones, see your life before you, from your birth to your death. Do not focus on the minutes and the seconds of this day. See the souls that will be paraded into hell some day because they did not respond to the grace that I am giving to them. I am sending you on a great mission. How you act, how you love in this world, will make the difference to many. See the big picture. Do not focus on the moments and the seconds in your life. Look, My dear one. Pray to the Spirit to open up your eyes and fill you with My grace. Where you are blind, you will now see.

8. **R.** The Presentation in the Temple is such an important mystery! Mary was told that a sword, too, would pierce her soul. All grace is released through Mary.

9. **Jesus:** Come unto Me, My beloved ones. I want to hold you gently in My arms and press you close to My Heart. I am Jesus. I speak to you with tenderness and love. You do not hear the gentle words that I speak to you, for you are busy and your lives are noisy. Release yourselves and come away with Me for short moments all through the day. Feel the presence of the Almighty God as I live and dwell within your hearts. I love you. I love you. I love you. I give to you now My abundant life. I am strengthening you for the days ahead. You are My soldiers that I will send to light up the dark night.

10. **R.** And she stands beneath the cross. I hear the wailing cries of the Virgin Mary as she sees her Son hang and suffer for three agonizing hours. She knows of the little children that will be condemned to hell forever, the little hearts that were willful, that did not accept the great grace that Jesus merited through His death.

The Finding of the Child Jesus in the Temple

1. **R.** The child Jesus was taken up to the Temple for the feast of Passover. Mary's Heart ached constantly from the prophecy of Simeon. Feel in your heart as Mary felt. She knew ever since

the prophecy of Simeon of the suffering to come. There was such a connection between Jesus and Mary, such intimacy between them! We see the Two Hearts beating within her body in the first two mysteries of the rosary. She provides life for Jesus through her milk in the third mystery. She comes to the Temple with the child Jesus in her arms and Simeon tells her of the sufferings to come. Now they take the child Jesus to the Temple. Jesus is separated from Mary and Joseph. Mary and Joseph go on their way and Jesus is left behind. When Mary realizes that the child Jesus was left behind, her Heart is in such sorrow! She returns to find the child Jesus.

2. **R.** I see all through the mysteries of the rosary the intimacy between Jesus and Mary. This separation was so painful to Mary, for she knew of the separation to come. When she found the child Jesus, she said to Him, "Son, why have you done this to us? Your father and I have been looking for you with great anxiety." In her Heart, she knew the sufferings of Jesus to come. In the windows in this chapel, across from the Finding of Jesus in the Temple, is the Death of Jesus on the Cross. This was a small separation between her and her child. She searched, she knew of the sufferings to come. She knew of a more drastic separation. He would be locked in the tomb. Her Heart was in such sorrow, for she knew far more than what we see.

3. **R.** Mary carried many things in her Heart. Few times we hear her speak. There was a secret between her and her Son all through Their lives.

4. **R.** A sword, too, shall pierce your Heart, O Mary. Our eternal life was merited by Christ's life and death on the cross. Water and blood poured forth from His pierced Heart. Life flows through Mary's pierced Heart to us for she is the Mediatrix of all graces. Our Mother, giving to us, dispensing to us this life. As she gave life to the physical body of Jesus, so she dispenses supernatural life to us.

5. **R.** We are being formed more and more in the spiritual womb of Mary, through the Holy Spirit, to be more and more like Jesus.

6. **Mary:** My dear little children, I am Mary, your Mother. I ask you to pray as you have never prayed before from your heart for all the little lost children in this world today. I stood under

the cross and I watched my Son as He suffered and died. This day, my dear ones, many of my children will be lost forever, for their hearts are willful and they go about their lives in sin. Jesus loves each and every child. I am the Mother of each child. I love each one of my children, your brothers. Will you pray from your hearts, my dear children? Pray for all the little lost children of this world. I am Mary, your Mother, and I am asking you this day to hear my words. I speak to you with this urgent request to pray as you have never prayed before.

7. **Mary:** My Heart was in such sorrow for the loss of my child! My Heart is sorrowing for the loss of so many this day. My dear little children, pray. Offer your days, each day, to the Father in union with the Holy Sacrifice of the Mass, in the Spirit, with all the angels and saints and souls in purgatory. Offer up all of your actions for the little children of this world who are suffering and in pain.

8. **Mary:** I am Mary, your Mother. I speak to you. This is an urgent request. Let go and come to the Heart of my Son. He will fill you with such love and you will go into this world. You will spread this love. Pray to the Father. Come to my Heart and dwell in my Heart. For I dwell in the Heart of my Son, and I will place you in the deepest recesses of His Heart. Pray to the Holy Spirit. My dear ones, when you are filled with the love of God, when you come from a place where your hearts are filled with love, you will give love to all in this world. When your hearts are sorrowing and in pain, come to the Almighty God. Spend quiet moments with Him, and let Him fill you with His love. My Son Jesus is waiting and waiting, minute by minute, second by second, for you to come. Come, my little children, to the Heart of my Son.

9. **Jesus:** Many are called, but few are chosen. You have been called to the house of My Mother to hear this message. I am Jesus, your beloved Savior. I speak to you, My dear ones, with a soft and gentle Heart, always a Heart that is filled with such love! Come to Me and I will give to you all that you need. This world is hurting and in pain, and I am sending you into the world as My soldiers to light the darkness. My dear little ones, this world has turned godless. You must focus on the Almighty God. Do not let Satan talk in your minds to divide you. Do not

harbor in your hearts any resentment or anger toward your brothers. Harboring this resentment and anger hurts your union with Me. Only a heart of love can properly unite with My Heart. I call you to holiness. I call you to open up your hearts and let Me enter. I will give to you My divine life and My divine love. I am Jesus. I talk to you gently and sweetly. Do you hear? It is in the quietness that you will hear My gentle voice. I am attentive to your every need, gently caring for each and every one of the tasks that you perform. I love you! I love you! I love you! Surrender, My dear ones, and know that I will never abandon you. I wait by the door of your heart. I wait, I wait, I wait. Will you open your heart and let Me in? Trade any bitterness for My divine love. I am Jesus, your beloved Savior. I gave My life for you. Will you love your hurting brothers for Me?

10. Hail Mary...

R. Mary said to tell you that She has called each and every person here. She wants you to answer this call. The time is urgent and this world is in need of your prayers. Come to her Son in the Eucharist and in front of the Tabernacle. It is there that He will instruct you in the ways He wants you to go. You are loved far beyond your comprehension. It is in Him that you will find peace and joy. He has all the answers for your life. Do not pick up your phones and complain and argue. Come to the Heart of Jesus and feel the peace that He gives to you. Feel the life that He outpours. He is the Almighty God and He has all the power. Amen.

Song: I come to you with greatest love...

The Seven Sorrows of Mary...

R. Jesus said, "I love you! I love you! I love you!" He wants hearts that are on fire for love of Him. He wants to hear from your lips the words of your love. He is waiting and longing and thirsting. He loves you personally. He loves you so much!

ROSARY MEDITATIONS
JULY 15, 1995
GLORIOUS MYSTERIES FOR CHILDREN

The Resurrection

1. **R.** See the picture of Jesus as He hangs on the cross, His withered body dead on the cross. See next to this the picture of Jesus as He rose from the tomb on the third day, victorious and covered in light. See so clearly in His hands and His feet the glorified wounds of Christ. This is our beloved Savior. He came to this world to save man from his sins and to give to him His divine life. We see so clearly, in His hands and His feet, these wounds.

2. **Jesus:** Let the little children come to Me. My dear ones, let the children come and pray, pray the rosary. I am sending you children to go into the land and tell other children about the love of God. Satan is pressing so hard on the youth! The youth are so open and thirsty! Older people many times are set in their ways. Children are young. They can hear about the love of God and change very quickly. Reach the children and the children will carry this message for many, many years.

3. **R.** Mary Magdalene went to the tomb. When she got there the stone had been rolled back. She began to cry . While she was crying, she saw a man she thought was a gardener. It was Jesus. She recognized Jesus. She was overjoyed to see Jesus.

4. **Jesus:** Father, forgive them for they know not what they do. Always on your lips should be words of forgiveness for your beloved brothers, for I came to show you the way. I forgave all those who persecuted Me. It is in loving God and loving one another that you will have peace, joy and love within your hearts.

5. **Jesus:** As you are in your hearts, so shall you be in this world. I call you to holiness, I call you to prayer. Let go and release yourself to Me.

6. **R.** Come, give me life, abundant life. I thirst to be with Thee.

7. **Mary:** I see before me the starved children of this world, their skinny little bodies. My dear ones, there is such suffering in this

world today. You hold back from talking about the love of God for fear of what people will think. See, My dear ones, see the men who will be paraded into the fires of hell for their willfulness. You must speak and tell all of the love of God. It is through these rosaries that I will touch many hearts.

8. **R.** Jesus appeared to the apostles in the upper room. The first time he appeared, Thomas was not with them. The second time, Thomas was with them. Thomas wanted to see the nail prints. Jesus said, "Blessed are those who have not seen and yet believe." (Jn 20:29)

9. **R.** We pray for faith. We ask God to help us believe, to strengthen our faith, for us not to look for signs and wonders, but rather to feel the Almighty God inside, His almighty presence within us.

10. **Jesus:** Let the little children come to Me. My beloved ones, I come to this earth to give you life. I love the little children. Their hearts are so pure and so gentle! This world is teaching mighty lessons, mighty lessons of evil. You must go out into the world and draw the little children to My Heart. I am calling you to bring the little children to Me.

The Ascension

1. **R.** Jesus gave to the apostles the power to baptize and to forgive sins. It is through baptism that we are made children of God and heirs of heaven. We partake in His divine life.

2. **R.** He lives in the hearts of men. He operates this day in the hearts of men. Jesus Christ came to this earth. He walked the earth, He suffered and He died. He rose on the third day. He ascended into heaven. But He leaves behind His apostles to carry out His mission in their lives.

3. **R.** The Incarnation goes on this day in the Church.

4. **R.** We are constantly being formed in the womb of the Virgin Mary to be more and more like Jesus. Dear Holy Spirit, transform us in the womb of the Virgin Mary, so that we may grow more and more in this likeness of our beloved Savior.

5. **Jesus:** There are so many pure and tender hearts in the little children of this world. The children this day are being taught such vile things! How people hold back! They do not talk about the love of God with reverence. My dear little ones, I am asking you to speak to the children. They do not realize that the children

need to receive this message of love. They listen to the messages themselves and tell their children so little. I am sending you into the world. I am sending you to talk to the children about the love of God.

6. **Jesus:** My soldiers are mighty soldiers. I am fortifying them with My special graces to carry this message to the youth.

7. **Jesus:** See before your eyes a group of children with their hearts filled with the love of God and singing. Dear ones, the children's hearts are open and pure. They can turn many children's hearts to the love of God. For they have not yet turned off their hearts, not yet turned their hearts to hearts of stone. Go to the children and tell them about the love I have for them. Tell them about the Eucharist. I ascended into heaven, but I remain with you this day, in My divinity and humanity, in the Holy Eucharist. And I remain in the hearts of men who are in the state of grace, in a very, very special way. Let the little children come to Me. Do you want the world to change? You must reach the children and the priests. You are My soldiers. It is through your example that this world will see the mighty lessons of My love.

8. **Jesus:** Mission, My dear ones, this is your mission. You were commissioned in baptism to carry out My life, death, and resurrection in your lives. Will you follow this calling? I am Jesus, your Savior. I am asking you to go forth to this Godless world with your banner held high, with the love of God across your breast.

   R. Jesus, Jesus, Jesus, You are my beloved Jesus. Let us shout it from the highest mountain and declare it from the rooftops. Jesus has died, He has risen and He will come again. He is alive, He is alive, He is alive. He lives this day.

9. **Jesus:** You make things so difficult! They are so simple! If you go to the scriptures, you see exactly what I am saying. I am saying the same thing here. If you read the Acts of the Apostles, you see how the apostles went from town to town and many were converted. It is through your efforts to spread this love of God that many will be converted. Let your hearts be fervent and on fire for the love of God. Reach the children and you will reach the world.

10. **R.** And He raised His arms and He ascended into heaven, but

He left behind the apostles to carry out His work.

Descent of The Holy Spirit on the Apostles

1. **R.** They were all gathered in an upper room, the apostles and the Virgin Mary. See the Virgin Mary. She is seated above the apostles (in the window). The Holy Spirit descends upon them in parted tongues of fire and their hearts are transformed from fear to fearlessness.

2. **R.** They are filled with such vibrancy and fire that they go out into the world to preach the Gospel message, the message of the love of God.

3. **R.** Let us meditate on the mystery of God's love. Let us put aside all of the distractions in our minds and focus only on His abundant love. He is outpouring to us such love in this room as we pray the rosary. Jesus Christ, the Son of God, remains in the tabernacle and longs to communicate with us. He wants to be so close to us! I know what He is saying this day. He tells me He longs to be so close to us! He is the sweetest and most tender lover and He is waiting and waiting by the door of our heart.

4. **Jesus:** I call you again to bring the children to Me. Have the children baptized in the Holy Spirit. Have the children pray to the Holy Spirit! Children need to have the courage to stand up for God in the circles wherein they mix this day. Many children are Godless. Many other children are mocked for professing the faith or making the sign of the cross or saying grace. Bring the children to Me and teach them about praying to the Holy Spirit. It is through the Holy Spirit that they will be transformed from fear to fearlessness. As the apostles carried out the Gospel message, so the children too will carry out the message of God's love.

5. **Jesus:** Many children sit idle all summer and are looking for things to do. Tell them to come to the Junior Shepherds of Christ prayer chapters. I want this movement spread throughout the world among the youth. This is My movement to touch the youth of this world.

6. **Jesus:** Circulate this rosary on the love of God and the love I have for My blessed, little ones.

7. *Song:* Come Holy Ghost...

8. **Jesus:** Do not worry about the circulation of these messages, for I am sending to you key people to help you to do this work.

You must remain fearless and unattached, surrendering and yielding. I am giving to you abundant graces to carry out this work. Surrender and let go and watch things happen around you. I am Jesus, your beloved Savior. My youth will march on this world with hearts filled with fire for the love of God.

9. **Jesus:** I will give to you rosaries such as these for children to use in the Junior Shepherds of Christ Movement. I want the children in this movement to have these meditations, to use them and to know exactly what I am telling them. I am Jesus. I will give the youth great graces to be drawn ever closer to My Heart through My Mother's Heart.

10. **Jesus:** Many are called, but few are chosen. I am calling My children to unite under the Junior Shepherds of Christ Movement and to carry this movement across the United States to children who are hurting and in pain. Many children this day are suffering far beyond your realization. I am Jesus. I am begging you to be open to all the children I send to you and to tell them about the Junior Shepherds of Christ Movement.

The Assumption of Our Lady

1. **R.** Mary is taken, body and soul, into heaven. She remained on the earth after the death of Jesus. Now she is taken to her final glory.

2. **R.** Mary remains as Mother of the Church and Mother of each one of us. She is by our side. She is with us, molding us and forming us in her womb, through the power of the Holy Spirit, to be more and more like her Son Jesus.

3. **Mary:** Go to the children now, My dear, dear ones. I am Mary, your mother. I am asking you to go out to the children. Many children will lose their souls and be condemned to the fires of hell. It is through your efforts to spread this movement, the Junior Shepherds of Christ, that these children will be saved from their own doom.

4. **Mary:** Little children's prayers are so powerful! I am Mary, your Mother. I am asking you to man the forces and have my little army of children ready and marching on this world with their pure little hearts and talking about the love of God. Children love to sing and they will love to pray when they know about the lives of my Son Jesus and myself, when you teach them about the Mass and the great gifts they are given.

Give to children the first Blue Book and let them hear the personal love letters my Son is delivering to them.

5. **Jesus:** You are missing a big source of your power by not contacting the children. When children pray, there is power. Children joined in numbers are a vital force for spreading this movement across the United States. Your land is a land that is very sick. It is in curing the children of their illnesses that your land will prosper.

6. **Mary:** Think of the little children coming to Mass and longing to receive my Son Jesus in the Holy Eucharist. Think of them coming with their little hearts and telling Jesus of their love. I am Mary, their Mother, and I want to rock them and hold them tenderly, close to my Heart, to rock them and cuddle them in my Heart. I love each precious little young child. Will you tell them for me? I am Mary, and I am calling you to reach out to the children.

7. **Mary:** Children are being taught at such an early age about sex, but they are not being taught about the love of God. I am Mary, your Mother. You must have courage to stand up and talk about the love of God. Think of how the children are being taught this day about all the vile things. People have the courage to stand up and spread such filth, but so few speak to the children about the burning love of my Son Jesus. How my Son Jesus loves the little children. **Jesus:** Let the little children come to Me.

8. **Mary:** I want this rosary to circulate among the children. I want you to encourage children to pray the rosary with these meditations. I want to tell the children how I love them with the tenderest, motherly love and how I am protecting them and guarding them and watching them. I am spreading My Motherly mantle over them. I am Mary, the Mother of Jesus and the mother of all the children of this world.

9. **Mary:** Think of how a mother loves her children. I love my children with the tenderest motherly love. Will you help me lead these tender young hearts to the Heart of my beloved Son, on fire for love of them? Many souls will be condemned to hell for their sinfulness and their willfulness. I am asking you to go out and to talk to the children about the love of my Son.

10. **Mary:** These rosary meditations and the Blue Books should be circulated among the children. I am asking you to carry the

Blue Book to the children and have them read it so they know how much Jesus, my Son, loves them.

The Crowning of Mary

1. **Mary:** The soul was created by God the Father to know and love God. Nothing on the face of this earth will feed the starved soul except the love of God. Make it clear to the children that their souls were created for the love of God. Their souls are hungry. They need to feed their souls with the love of God.

2. **R.** Mary was crowned Queen of Heaven and Earth. We, too, some day, if we love God and love each other, will be given a place in heaven far beyond our comprehension. We cannot understand the immensity of the love of God. Jesus Christ came to this earth. He was born a little baby. He suffered and died. He rose on the third day and ascended into heaven. He wants us to be with Him forever and ever in heaven.

3. **Mary:** The ways of this world are very evil ways. The little children are being taught young such evilness! I am your Mother. I am calling out to you to carry out this mission, for the children need to know the love of my Son. You will be given great graces to reach the children. You must know that Satan will press very hard to try to stop any efforts that you may make in trying to reach the children. I am Mary, your Mother, and I am protecting you with my motherly mantle.

4. **Mary:** If you instruct the children, as I have instructed you, on the lives of Jesus and Mary, they will love to pray the rosary.

5. **Jesus:** It is through the Junior Shepherds of Christ Movement that I will reach the youth throughout this world.

6. **Mary:** Children every day need to consecrate their hearts to the Sacred Heart of Jesus and the Immaculate Heart of Mary.

7. **Jesus:** When you are tired and weary, know that Satan is pressing on you. You are receiving abundant graces to carry out this work. I will see to the publishing of these messages. You must release yourself and pray as you have never prayed before. Pray that the Father will answer your prayers. Pray in union with the Holy Sacrifice of the Mass, through the intercession of the Sorrowful Mother.

8. **Mary:** I am so sorrowful for the little lost children of this world, for the slaughter of the little innocent babies within the womb of their mothers, for the slaughter of the minds of children in

many classrooms. I am Mary, your Mother. Speak out, pray for the courage from the Holy Spirit to speak out for the love of God. If this world can talk about so many vile things, if it shows movies in the movie theaters where Satan is coming out of the screen, my dear ones, you can surely talk about the tender, burning Heart of my Son Jesus.

9. **Mary:** Many young hearts will be converted and, in that conversion, the power of their prayers will be magnified far beyond your comprehension. I am Mary, your Mother. This is a rosary given from the Hearts of Jesus and Mary on July 15, 1995. This is a call to reach the children in the Junior Shepherds of Christ Movement, to bring them to my Immaculate Heart, that they may be consecrated in my Heart and consecrated in the Heart of my Son.

10. **Mary:** Tell the children to pray to my Son and the Holy Spirit for the courage to go into this world, for they are fighting a battle every day in this world and my Son will reward them with abundant grace and great gifts of His tender love. I am Mary, your Mother. I have called out to you. Harken to my call and tell all involved of my request here. I love you, my sweet little children, and I love the little children of the world. Let the little children come to my Son Jesus and let them forever rest in His burning Heart of love.

Song: Little child, little child, come and rest in My arms. Be with Me, little child, I want you with Me, you are hurting, My loved one. I am waiting for you, come into My Heart now. I love you.

ROSARY MEDITATIONS
JULY 28, 1995
THE SORROWFUL MYSTERIES

The Agony in the Garden

1. **Jesus:** My dear ones, I am Jesus and you must listen to the words that I am speaking to you, for I am telling you that sufferings at this time are befalling this earth and that Satan is pressing down. He is pressing down so hard on all My beloved, faithful ones! As you see the confusion, the doubt, and the troubles mount in your life at this moment, you will know that Satan is

busy and his work is at hand. I am molding you as special soldiers to go into this world to spread My love. How dearly I love
each of you. I have called you here to pray this rosary with all
your heart. Let your heart be open; let your heart be soft.

Let Me fill you with My love so you feel within you My
burning love. Although the earth be shaken and not give its
light, you will know that the Almighty God dwells within your
heart and that you have nothing to fear, for a graced soul is constantly filled with the presence of the Father, the Son and the
Holy Spirit. I am Jesus, your beloved Savior. You do not know
the tricks and the handiwork that Satan has planned to stop My
faithful ones from spreading My love. It is in focusing on My
burning Heart, My Heart of deepest love, that you will withstand all the trials with joy in your heart for, minute by minute,
second by second, I am present with you. I am with you at this
very moment. You are telling every person you meet about the
God who lives within you. Let your hearts be filled with joy for
I am truly present and in your midst. I am Jesus Christ, the Son
of God, in this room with you in the tabernacle, the same as the
day I walked the earth and died on the cross. Let your hearts be
joyous. Rejoice and give thanks to the Almighty God and praise
His name, for you are called, you are favored, you are chosen
and you are loved with My deepest, burning love.

2. **Jesus:** In the garden I knelt with such agony in My Heart, for in
   My divine knowing I saw before Me all of the events about to
   happen. I knew of every beating, all of the blood that I would
   shed, but, more than anything, I knew the rejection and pain in
   My Heart for the love I had for My beloved ones and how they
   would reject Me. Look at your world this day. It was in the garden that I suffered for all of the souls that have forgotten God. I
   cry out to you from the tabernacle to realize My presence with
   you. You are given great gifts in this room. I want you to unite
   closely to My Heart, for I am longing and thirsting and waiting
   for this love affair with you. This rosary will be a time when you
   will share My deepest love. I am giving you great graces when
   you come before Me in the tabernacle. I will draw you more
   and more closely to My Heart. As I suffered in the garden for
   the souls that beat Me and treated Me with indifference, I was
   comforted by the acts of love that you are giving to Me this day.

3. **R.** The eyes of Jesus that cried bloody tears for all of the souls that have forgotten Him! Jesus calls from the tabernacle. Constantly I hear His lamenting cry of how He longs and thirsts to be ever closer to the hearts of men. Many men have turned their backs and do not realize the gentleness and sweetness of His love.

4. **Jesus:** Love is giving, My dear ones, giving of yourself for the sake of others. Many this day do not know the meaning of love. To love means to give of yourself, to give for the other. Many times it is hard to love and keep giving love for, as you are self-giving, the other continues to be selfish, but I am calling you to love. As you meditate on this passion, focus on My love, given for all, how I was persecuted and suffered and still loved. My way is love. Focus on the meaning of the word love and what it means to you.

5. **Jesus:** I am vigilant and forever by your side. Unconditionally I love you. No matter what you have done in your life, I love you.

6. **Jesus:** It is this love that I want you to give to this world. Love is giving.

7. **Jesus:** My love is gentle. My love is sweet. My love is kind.

8. **Jesus:** I give to you great graces to help you to love in this world that is hurting and in pain. Satan will cause confusion and division in your lives. He will tempt and tempt you to try to justify your actions. You must be silent many times, and yield and pray, for he is trying to create great division in your lives. You must go to My Heart and take refuge there and focus on My love for you. You are My soldiers that I am sending into this world to spread My love. Will you answer this call? Will you pray for more and more grace to spread this love to a world that is hurting and in pain?

9. **Jesus:** Think of how it is when you love someone so much and that person walks by and ignores you. Your heart is crying out for union with that person but in his coldness he does not see you and goes his way. My dear ones, his heart is in pain and hurting. I came to show you the way of love. My way is love. When your brother mistreats you, you must realize that within he is hurting and in pain.

10. **Jesus:** I come to give you peace, peace in your hearts and in

your souls. Do not argue with your brothers. When you argue, Satan is there trying to cause division. I am asking you to focus always on the love in My Heart. I am giving you messages of My love. Do you realize the great gifts that you are given, that you are in this room, in this chapel, in the presence of the Almighty God? Focus on the great gifts given to you this day from the Almighty God.

How can you be glum and sad in your ways when you realize that the Almighty God loves you with the deepest love and that He is present. Pray for the grace to see more and more, for many are blind and do not see the great gifts given to them. I am giving to you, My faithful ones, great gifts and the graces to see with much clarity. Open your heart and pray for the grace to love your brothers as I have loved you.

Satan wants you focused on yourself so you will not spread the light to this world that is hurting and in pain. Satan wants souls for hell—souls for hell! Do you realize that? Let go of any kind of selfishness that you feel within yourself and vow to love and to give. Let go, release. If you let go you will feel tremendous freedom and My grace will pour into your heart and you will be filled with My burning love.

Jesus Is Scourged at the Pillar

1. **Jesus:** You do not know the extent to which Satan will go to keep you focused on yourselves. He is busy and working hard to keep your hearts set on problems. I am Jesus and I am giving you My abundant love. Focus on My love for you.

2. **Jesus:** You are My lights that I am sending into this world to spread My love. It is the smile on your face, the look in your eye, the gentleness in your voice, the love that you give to this world in all the little actions that will send My message of love to those you touch. Let go and surrender and pray for grace. Whatever is bothering you, let go and you will feel an outpouring of My grace as it rushes into your heart and you are set free, for minute by minute, second by second, Father, Son and Holy Spirit dwell within you and you are never alone. If the earth is shaken and the sun ceases to shine, you will have this presence of the Almighty God firmly fixed within your heart.

3. **Jesus:** They tore My flesh; they beat My body. See My body, dear ones, covered with wounds and bleeding. See the wounds,

deep wounds, My flesh torn open by the angry hearts of these men! I came to show you the way. In all of this torture I loved those who tore open My flesh. I came to show you the way to love. I ask you this day to release anything that is hurting inside of you, and you will feel joy in your heart, for to know Me is to have joy in your heart. Amidst all the sufferings that you are going through, keep your focus on Me.

4. **Jesus:** Your life is a constant reliving of death-resurrection. My dear ones, as you suffer this day, as you stay rooted in Me, you are brought to deeper and deeper life in Me. You live this paschal mystery of death-resurrection in your daily lives. I came to show you the way. I came to show you the way to love. Love is gentle, love is kind. It is caring for the other. In this world today many hearts have turned cold.

5. **Jesus:** In the intensity of My deepest love I want you to feel the vibrancy of this love within your heart. At this moment, focus on the presence of the Father, your loving Father who created you with such preciousness and such beauty. He created you, a very unique part of His plan, a plan for the salvation of the world. There is not another person who is like you, and He dwells within your heart. When you are in the state of grace, the Father, the Son and the Holy Spirit live within you.

6. **Jesus:** Come to the Heart of My Mother. Lay yourself down in her Heart and be cradled by her love. As you dwell in her Heart, so too will you dwell in My Heart. Feel this presence, of dwelling within the Heart of your loving Mother and dwelling within My Heart, on fire for love of you!

7. **Jesus:** The Holy Spirit, who proceeds from the mutual love of the Father and of the Son, is present within you, My dear ones. Do you feel His fire and His vibrancy as He leads you more and more on your way, on this journey to eternity?

8. **Jesus:** My dear ones, focus now on the presence of the Almighty God within you, of the Father, and His love for you, of the Son and Holy Spirit. Feel the security. You have nothing to fear. The only fear that you should have is for the loss of the life in your soul. Let go, surrender, and feel the freedom of knowing the presence of the Almighty God that lives in a graced soul.

9. **Jesus:** Tremendous gifts you are given, My beloved ones. Pray

for the grace to realize the gifts that you are given. I stood at the pillar and they tore My flesh. The men, with their angry hearts and ugly faces, with hatred deep-rooted in their hearts. I shed My blood for them. I loved these men, these men that put me to My death. See Me wounded, with deep wounds that ripped My flesh. I am with you at every second. You receive abundant graces for loving when others are cold to you. I am with you every second. Let go and surrender. The time is at hand. Many souls will be lost and I am calling you to go into this world to spread My message of love. I am Jesus. I love you, I love you, I love you. From the tabernacle I call out to you with My Heart, yearning with deepest love, wounded for all the souls that have forgotten and treat Me with such indifference. Think of someone you love walking by and ignoring you. I am ignored and forgotten, treated with disrespect. I am, My dear ones, the Son of God! I wait, I wait, I wait for My beloved ones to come and, from their lips, to whisper their words of love. I am a Person and I am longing and thirsting for your love. Open your hearts and come to Me.

10. Hail Mary…

Jesus is Crowned with Thorns

1. **Jesus:** The words that wound! Words from your beloved brother! Do you see My body, covered with wounds, wounds all over My body? When your brother treats you with ugliness, My dear ones, focus on the wounds covering My body and pray for the grace to act as I would want you to act.

2. **Jesus:** My dear ones, let your hearts be in joy as you realize My presence continually within you. During all of your sufferings, I am with you.

3. **R.** They pounded into His head a sharp crown of piercing thorns. Look at the head of Jesus, punctured by the thorns, the deep holes around His forehead. Focus on these wounds and then think of the little wounds that we receive, the words spoken, the problems that we let press on our minds. Look at Jesus and think of the crown of thorns pressing on His head. He allows us to suffer and in this suffering we are brought to greater and greater life in Him. Do we feel this divine life within us?

4. **R.** Look at the crowned head of Jesus and see the blood that comes down His face and goes into His eyes and into His ears.

His hands were tied. He could not even try to wipe the blood from His brow. He loved those men that crowned Him with thorns.

5. **Jesus:** You will suffer much mental persecution this day, a pressing down of problems and things in your life that will irritate you. You must focus on My love for you. Come and dwell in the Heart of My Mother and, when you dwell in her Heart, you will dwell deeply in My Heart. You must come for our love. Things will be very hard and you will not be able to withstand the trials without Our love.

6. **Jesus:** Why do you go it alone when I am here, I am present, and I am outpouring My life, My grace, to you this day. Let go, surrender. When you are backed up against a wall, let go. I am here. Trust. (**R.** Jesus, I trust in You.) Forever on your lips say, "Dear Sacred Heart of Jesus, I trust in You!"

7. **Jesus:** Accept all that is going on in your life this day for I am allowing these trials to strengthen you for the days ahead. The trials you are experiencing will strengthen you.

8. **Jesus:** Praise the Almighty God for the great gifts that you are given in these sufferings for you are growing more and more in My life. They pounded into My head a sharp crown of piercing thorns and in all of this I remained at peace, for I knew that it was the Father's Will. Surrender and let go. I am with you, second by second, minute by minute. I ponder the way of your heart and I am with you.

9. **Jesus:** You too can have joy in suffering if you realize the presence of the Almighty God. I am allowing this suffering to help you grow in your graced life.

10. **Jesus:** I love you, I love you, I love you. Surrender and let go, for I am truly with you.

Jesus Carries His Cross Up Calvary

1. **Jesus:** I ask you to carry the cross that you are given this day and to carry this cross with joy in your heart.

2. *Song:* See the eyes that look at Mary…

3. **R.** Jesus' and Mary's eyes met on the way to Calvary. Jesus looked into the face of His beloved Mother and He saw the tender love, and the hurt in her face. Mary looked into the eyes of Her Son and she knew of the suffering that He was undergoing. She saw His physical strain. She saw Him fall under the cross.

She saw His blood and His wounds. She saw, in the meeting of their eyes, the immense love that He has for us this day.

4. **R.** It is in Mary that we will reach this deep intimacy with the Heart of Jesus. It is in going to Mary's Heart, in being rocked in her arms and held close to her breast, that she gives to us the milk of salvation. She gives to us life from her Son Jesus.

5. **R.** It is in knowing the tender love of our beloved Mother that we will join more deeply to the love of Father, Son and Holy Spirit. It is through Mary's Heart that we are carried to this love of God.

6. **Jesus:** Release yourself and let go for I am truly present in this room with you at this very moment. Put off all distractions. Focus more and more on My presence with you. All through your day, all through your encounters with others, I want you to be aware of My presence with you, not just when you pray, but all through the day—when you are talking to others, when you are walking, whatever you are doing.

7. **R.** Be alone in a room and be aware of the immense love within your being of Father, Son and the Holy Spirit. You are touched so deeply within your soul! In this time you sit with the Father, Son, and Holy Spirit and you soak in this presence. Time passes by, but you are unaware, for you are lost in this experience with the presence of God. Time stands still.

At this point you rise and walk from the room. As you walk from the room, you know that your heart has been touched deeply by the presence of the Almighty God, Father, Son and Holy Spirit. You walk into a new world, for you are free of anxiety. You have been touched in such a way that you know that the Almighty God is truly present and living within you. You know that you do not have to fear, for the power and might of God are truly within you. You walk from this room and you carry this special touch of grace with you throughout the day. And, although the earth is shaken and the sun ceases to shine, you are steadfast in His love and His presence.

Jesus: My dear ones, things will begin to happen. So much confusion and doubt now in your life! Sufferings are coming. You must know this presence within you. It is in this presence, with the Almighty God within you, that you will have deep joy within your heart at all times for you know what God is telling you.

You know that He is inside of you. You can watch things fall down around you, and people stumble in your midst, but you know that, if you stay steadfastly fixed in the love of Almighty God, you do not fear for He is truly present. You walk from this room and, as you walk, you carry this presence with you. Wherever you go, know that you have been touched by a special grace and that the presence of the Almighty God–Father, Son, and Holy Spirit–truly dwells within you. Your greatest fear is to lose the life of God by sin. Everything else will work according to the plan of the Father if you surrender and carry this presence within you. Do His Will.

8. **R.** And the earth was shaken, and trees fell, and many catastrophes hit the land, but within their hearts there was an inner peace and tranquillity as they walked from the room, for they were touched by Almighty God. Nothing can shake the presence of God within their hearts.

9. **R.** And He carried the cross on His back. His body was stooped over, and His face was covered with blood, and His head crowned with thorns, and He could hardly move. He fell three times under the weight of the cross but within His Heart was peace for He knew the love of His Father. He knew the Father's Will. You, too, will go about your life and have peace and joy within your heart, for you will know that as you walk the Almighty God dwells within you.

Jesus: Be one with Me, My precious ones, one with Me. Unite more and more to Me. Say the Prayer for Union with Me. Every day pray this prayer. Let go, surrender and feel the freedom of knowing the indwelling of the Trinity.

10. **Jesus:** As you see My face covered with blood, see My body stooped down and the cross on My back. I could hardly move. As you look into My eyes, tender, loving eyes, My dear ones, I want you to hear three words from My lips as I look back at you with My tender loving eyes. I love you!

Jesus is Crucified and Dies on the Cross

1. **R.** Jesus was raised high on the cross on Calvary. See Him on the hill and see Mary under the cross and hear the wind blow. See the cross against the darkened sky. This is the greatest sacrifice: the Son of God gave His all to the Father for love of us. His hands were pierced, His feet were pierced, His head was

crowned with thorns. He surrendered and gave His life that we might have life forever with Him in heaven.

2. **R.** As you go to each Mass, unite in oneness with the priest, the priest who is Christ present at the Mass. Unite in this oneness and offer yourself in this act of self-giving to the Father. See Jesus at the Last Supper as He offered the bread and hear His words, "…this is my body" (Mk 14:22), for He knew He would give His flesh and His blood for the love of His precious souls. At Mass we offer ourselves, through and with Christ, to the Father, in the Holy Spirit.

3. **R.** It is in uniting ourselves to the Holy Sacrifice of the Mass being offered all through the world at every moment, offering ourselves with this sacrifice to the Father, that this is our most powerful prayer and that our prayers are magnified to such an extent. All through the day offer, with the Holy Sacrifice of the Mass, to the Father, in the Holy Spirit, through the intercession of the Virgin Mary. Offer up, My dear ones, your prayers–for the souls suffering in this world this day, for the souls in Purgatory that need your prayers–all of your petitions. Unite them to the Holy Sacrifice of the Mass going on constantly, the greatest prayer that you can give to the Father.

4. **Jesus:** This is My Body. This is My Blood.

5. **Jesus:** My dear ones, I give you Myself this day in the Holy Sacrifice of the Mass, and you take this so lightly. As I gave Myself as a sacrifice on Calvary, so I give Myself to you this day. Deeper and deeper My union with you grows as you receive Me in the Eucharist. I am crying out to you to realize the great gifts that you are given, for, when you receive Me in the Eucharist, you become so united in such oneness with Me.

6. **Jesus:** Prepare yourself for this event. Prepare to receive the Almighty God in deepest union in your heart and pray for the grace that this Mass will be filled with meaning for you and that you will unite in such oneness with Me. You pray at the Offertory to the Father that He accept this Sacrifice. Offer your lives to the Father with Me. Put your life in His hands. Let Him run your life and you will be free and good will happen for you, as you grow more and more in your life and unite more and more closely to Him.

7. **Jesus:** As you unite in such oneness with Me, you unite also

with all those present in Me. **R.** Let the world unite in the Holy Sacrifice of the Mass, and all become one in Christ, for we are one body in Him and He is the head.

8. **R.** Let us all pray in union with the Holy Sacrifice of the Mass throughout the world and offer ourselves up continually in this Sacrifice with Jesus to the Father. As we all do this there will be unity in this offering, for we are all one in Him. As we unite in Him, we unite in each other.

9. **R.** Ave Maria! It is through the pierced Heart of Jesus that the sacramental life of the Church was born. Blood and water flowed forth from His Heart–water, the symbol of baptism, our rebirth in Him, and blood, the symbol of the Eucharist, whereby we are fed by his Body. As the life flows through His pierced Heart, so it flows through His beloved Mother, for her Heart was invisibly pierced with a sword and she is the Mediatrix of all grace. As she nourished the Christ Child within her womb, so she provides the life to us from her Son Jesus through her spiritual womb.

10. **R.** I see the life flow from His pierced Heart, through the Heart of the Virgin Mary, and into our hearts. We are saturated with this divine life and divine love. It is from His Heart that all mercy and love flow.

"MEDITATING ON THE ROSARY AVES"
A collection of meditations previously published as a set

I. THE JOYFUL MYSTERIES

The Annunciation

1. **R.** The Angel Gabriel appeared to Mary and asked her to be the mother of the Messiah.

2. **R.** She said yes. Mary had such faith! She always complied with the Father's Will.

3. **R.** She was filled with the Holy Spirit, and the Word was made flesh and dwelt among us.

4. **R.** There was such a bond between Jesus and Mary from the very moment of conception!

5. **R.** She felt His life grow within her womb. His Most Sacred

Heart was formed in her womb through the Holy Spirit.

6. **R.** Jesus wants to be alive in our hearts. We should carry His life with great joy in our being.

7. **R.** The Spirit wants to be alive in our very being with the fire of His love.

8. **R.** We are children of God. Mary mothers us as she mothered Jesus.

9. **R.** It is through Mary that we are led to intense love in His most precious Heart.

10. **R.** It is truly the love of these Two Hearts that will lead us to union with God.

The Visitation

1. **R.** Mary went to visit her cousin Elizabeth.

2. **R.** When she arrived, the child in Elizabeth's womb leapt for joy at the presence of Mary with Jesus in her womb.

3. **R.** Mary was filled with the Holy Spirit and cried out, with a loud voice, the Magnificat.

4. **R.** "My soul proclaims the greatness of the Lord and my spirit rejoices in God my Savior." (Lk 1:46,47)

5. **R.** "…because He has looked upon the humiliation of his servant. Yes, from now onwards all generations will call me blessed." (Lk 1:48)

6. **R.** God who is mighty has done great things to us in His name.

7. **R.** Jesus is no less present in our hearts after Communion than He was in Mary's womb.

8. **R.** Should we not jump up and cry out that we truly receive the one, true God in our hearts?

9. **R.** Are we open to the Holy Spirit to fill us with the love of the one, true God and Mary in our hearts?

10. **R.** It is through her pure and tender Heart that we will love God more closely.

The Birth of Jesus

1. **R.** Joseph was filled with joy to see the splendor of the night, but with sorrow to see Jesus born in such poverty.

2. **R.** Not a place for Jesus to lay His head—in a manger at birth, His head on a cross at His death—both bare wood.

3. **R.** He showed us the way, in total submission to the will of the Father. He loved us so much that He was born a human, God-made-man.

4. **R.** What the birth of this baby, the child Jesus, did to change the world for all time!

5. **R.** This is Jesus, the Son of God, come to free the world of its sins.

6. **R.** He came as a little baby. He was born of Mary in the little town of Bethlehem.

7. **R.** This is how it is with Jesus today: there is no blare of trumpets, no roll of drums. Jesus comes quietly at every Mass.

8. **R.** The only blare of trumpets and roll of drums are in our hearts.

9. **R.** If you are not aware of Christ truly present in the Eucharist, you miss the big event.

10. **R.** Jesus, the same Jesus who was born in Bethlehem, comes to us in our hearts.

The Presentation of Jesus in the Temple

1. **R.** Mary took Jesus to the temple to be presented to the Father.

2. **R.** Simeon told Mary of the future sufferings of Jesus and Mary.

3. **R.** Joseph, in his sorrow at hearing of the sufferings, was comforted by the joy that so many souls would be redeemed.

4. **R.** They returned to Galilee to the town of Nazareth and Jesus grew in wisdom and strength.

5. **R.** Mary, with such love, beheld her precious Son!

6. **R.** She gazed into His precious Baby eyes.

7. **R.** Simeon predicted that her Heart would be pierced with a sword.

8. **R.** Her Heart would be pierced with a sword for, just as she held His baby body at birth, she would hold his lifeless body under the cross.

9. **R.** How well Mary would know the Heart of Jesus! She would ponder all the events of His life in her Heart.

10. **R.** It is through her most loving Heart that we grow in fervent love for His Heart.

The Finding of Jesus in the Temple

1. **R.** When Jesus was twelve years old, the Holy Family went to Jerusalem for Passover.

2. **R.** When it was over Mary and Joseph had traveled a day's journey before they realized Jesus was not with them.

3. **R.** With sorrow in their hearts they returned to Jerusalem to find Him.

4. **R.** After searching for Him for three days, they found Him in the temple talking to the doctors.
5. **R.** The doctors were astounded at His wisdom.
6. **R.** He said He had to be about His Father's business.
7. **R.** Jesus teaches us today through His word.
8. **R.** He went down and was subject to them.
9. **R.** Mary, if we ever lose Jesus, lead us back to His tender Heart.
10. **R.** Jesus, help us to love Mary more.

THE SORROWFUL MYSTERIES

The Agony in the Garden

1. **R.** Agonies of the heart are the greatest of all agonies. How Jesus suffered for all who would treat Him so coldly!
2. **R.** He who loves us so perfectly, with a Heart on fire for us, is treated with such indifference!
3. **R.** His Heart is an open furnace. He calls out to us, "I love you so dearly. Please, My children, please come and give your love to Me!"
4. **R.** In the garden He saw before Him all the people from all time who would not even think of Him, day after day after day, and still He loved them so much!
5. **R.** He waits for us to come and be with Him in the Eucharist. So many people receive Him and do not talk to Him!
6. **R.** He agonized over all the souls who would suffer eternal damnation despite His Sacrifice for their salvation.
7. **R.** He saw before Him all the suffering He would undergo for deepest love of us and in compliance with His Father's will.
8. **Mary:** I am the Immaculate Heart. If only you knew, my dear children, how much my Son loves you!
9. **R.** His Heart was in such sorrow and anguish! We do not know even now how much this Heart suffered for love of us! He thirsts for the love of souls.
10. **R.** He asks us to tell Him how much we truly love Him.

The Scourging at the Pillar

1. **R.** Jesus loved Judas dearly but Judas betrayed Jesus with a kiss.
2. **R.** Jesus stood by. They hit His face. They pulled His hair. They treated Him so cruelly!

3. **R.** His beloved mother stood by and watched her once-small-child suffer so! But she was helpless and could not raise a hand.
4. **R.** They tied Him to a pillar.
5. **R.** His tender back was beaten so brutally that flesh now hung from His body.
6. **R.** The blood ran down His precious skin from His head to His toes.
7. **R.** With mean hearts and angry faces they whipped Jesus with horrible instruments.
8. **R.** As He stood there absorbing this punishment He thought of us and how He loves us so dearly.
9. **R.** He thought of our brothers, too. He loves them with the same intense love.
10. **R.** As He suffered so from the sins of men He was comforted by the acts of love we give to Him this very day.

The Crowning with Thorns

1. **R.** They clothed Him with a dirty, purple robe and mocked Him as king.
2. **R.** They pounded the crown of thorns onto His most precious head.
3. **R.** The blood ran down, bright red blood, into His eyes and into His ears.
4. **R.** Put yourself there and watch Jesus as He is crowned with thorns and people holler such horrible things!
5. **R.** Jesus sits with His head down like a little lamb about to be led to the slaughter.
6. **R.** Think of how it would be to have someone taunt and assault you.
7. **Jesus:** "They wounded My head with a crown of thorns and I bled for love of you."
8. **Jesus:** "My children, do you know how I love you? I love you this very day."
9. **R.** He would suffer for us this very day.
10. **Jesus:** "Come to Me in the Eucharist. I long for your love. I am He Who shed His blood for you."

The Carrying of the Cross

1. **R.** See Jesus stand there as they condemned Him to death—the hate and anger on their faces while Jesus stood, bound like a criminal, with a look of peace on His face, at peace because He

knew the Father's love.

2. **Jesus:** When they holler and persecute you, see My love given for you. See Me with My body beaten and battered. See My Father as He loves you this very day. Know that you are loved.

3. **R.** Mary walked the whole way by His side.

4. **R.** Do we know even a little of how the Heart of Mary ached as she watched her Son beaten and poked as He fell to the ground with the cross on His back. She had to stand helplessly by and not say a word.

5. **R.** Do we see the love that Jesus and Mary have for us? Do we see that they are always with us, loving us so much? Or do we wander our own way, thinking no one loves us?

6. **R.** He falls under the cross, then rises, again and again. This is the love He has for us.

7. **R.** They peered into each other's eyes. "This is the love We give to you. Would you listen to Us, please?"

8. **R.** His Heart beat, even to its last, for love of us, but we do not think of how much love God has for each of us this very day.

9. **R.** Always complying with the will of the Father, He plodded on as they led Him to the hill of Calvary.

10. **R.** Veronica wiped the face of Jesus, that beautiful face, once so unblemished, now covered with blood.

The Crucifixion and Death of Jesus

1. **R.** She stood by and watched the same hands—once gentle, baby hands—now hammered with big nails.

2. **R.** She saw His feet—those little feet she once held—now hammered with big nails.

3. **R.** She watched as His skin—that tender skin she cared for as she babied Him—was now all battered, torn, bruised and bloodied!

4. **R.** And she calls out to us this day: "This is my Son. This is how He loves you. What more do you want Him to do to show you His love?"

5. **R.** He remains with us in the Eucharist with such love! He gave Himself on the cross. He gives Himself to us this very day.

6. **Mary:** I saw what He suffered because He loved you so. I suffered by His side. I call out to you. I am your beloved mother. Come to Him.

7. **Mary:** His Heart is on fire for love of you today.

8. **Mary:** Stand under the cross with me and watch my Son die

such a terrible death!

9. **Mary:** Sit under the cross with me. Receive His lifeless body.
10. **Mary:** I am the Immaculate Heart of Mary and I cry out to you to spread His love to all of your brothers. For I come to tell you this day that He loves you so much and He loves your brothers and wants them to know this love. This is my call to you: to spread this love throughout this world.

THE GLORIOUS MYSTERIES

The Resurrection
1. **R.** On the third day He arose as he foretold.
2. **R.** When Mary Magdalen and some other women arrived at the tomb, they saw that the entry stone had been rolled away.
3. **R.** There appeared two men in dazzling garments where Jesus had been laid.
4. **R.** The two angels told the women He had risen as He had foretold.
5. **R.** He went to Emmaus and recounted for them all the scriptures, from Moses through the prophets, which referred to Him.
6. **R.** When He had seated Himself with them to eat, He took bread, pronounced the blessing, then broke the bread and began to distribute it to them. With that their eyes were opened and they recognized Him, whereupon He vanished from their sight.
7. **R.** He appeared several times to the apostles over the course of 40 days and gave them the power to baptize and forgive sins.
8. **R.** Christ died to bring us to new life.
9. **R.** He came that we might have life to the full.
10. **R.** The good news is that Jesus has died and that He has risen.

The Ascension
1. **R.** They went out of the town of Bethany and Jesus gave them his final blessing.
2. **R.** He raised His arms and ascended into heaven.
3. **R.** They stood below in utter amazement at what had happened.
4. **R.** Think of what it would be like to see Jesus ascend bodily into heaven.
5. **R.** Imagine the grief in Mary's and the apostles' hearts to see

Him go!

6. **R.** Jesus has not left. He remains with us in His divinity and humanity in the Eucharist today.

7. **R.** He longs for us to come and receive Him. He waits for us to come and be with Him in front of the tabernacle.

8. **R.** He gave Himself on the cross. He gives Himself this very day in the Eucharist.

9. **R.** He loved us so much He died for us. He rose to give us new life. As He ascended into heaven he left behind the most precious gift of all–Himself!

10. **R.** He said, "John baptised with water but, not many days from now, you are going to be baptised with the Holy Spirit." (Acts 1:5)

The Descent of the Holy Spirit

1. **R.** The apostles were full of fear and locked themselves in the Upper Room.

2. **R.** When the Holy Spirit descended on Mary and the apostles, what joy for Mary's Heart!

3. **R.** Jesus had promised to send the Holy Spirit. A great wind blew and over their heads appeared parted tongues of fire.

4. **R.** They were all filled with the Holy Spirit and began to speak in foreign tongues.

5. **R.** What joy for Mary to see the apostles transformed from fear to fearlessness!

6. **R.** Oh, Holy Spirit, come to us and fill our hearts with the fire of Your love.

7. **R.** Where we are full of fear, make us fearless.

8. **R.** We long to have the courage to do all God asks of us. Oh, Holy Spirit, give us this courage.

9. **R.** Holy Spirit, lead us to intimate oneness with You, the Father, the Son and Mary.

10. **R.** Oh, Holy Spirit, set us on fire for love of God.

The Assumption of Our Lady into Heaven

1. **R.** Many years after Jesus' death Mary was taken up to heaven.

2. **R.** Imagine her delight to be forever united with her most precious Son.

3. **R.** Imagine her joy to be united with the Father and the Holy Spirit. She beheld the face of God.

4. **R.** She had lived her whole life in service of Him. Now she was

taken up to her eternal dwelling place.

5. **R.** Mary has not left. She remains forever with us. She is wherever Jesus is. She is our spiritual mother. She is forever by our side. She loves us. She mothers us with such motherly love!

6. **R.** Who are we to have Mary as our mother?

7. **R.** Mary watched it all. A young Mary, an older Mary, a sad Mary, a joyful Mary—Mary, the reflection of Christ's life!

8. **R.** To know Christ is to see Him through Mary's eyes, to feel Him through Mary's motherhood, to love Him through Mary's Heart.

9. **R.** She forever intercedes for her beloved children. She cares for our every need.

10. **R.** Heaven is our true home.

The Coronation of Our Lady

1. **R.** A great sign appeared in the sky, a woman clothed with the sun, with the moon under her feet and on her head a crown of twelve stars.

2. **R.** Mary was crowned queen of heaven and earth. Our most beloved mother now reigns in the court of heaven!

3. **R.** Imagine her joy to hear the choirs of angelic voices! Imagine her joy to see the angels and saints praising God!

4. **R.** She—who carried the baby Jesus in her womb, who held Him in her arms, who walked by His side during the Passion, who stood under His cross, who held His lifeless body and watched Him locked in the tomb—was now crowned Queen of Heaven, forever to reign in the court of heaven with her beloved Son.

5. **R.** If we remain faithful to the Lord until death, we too will receive a crown of life. In heaven shall be found every good.

6. **R.** Such treasures for us in heaven! The eye has not seen, the ear has not heard the glories that await him who serves the Lord!

7. **R.** Heaven is the kingdom of God. We are His heirs.

8. **R.** There is no more thirsting for union with God, no more longing for Him. We will experience such intense union with Him forever.

9. **R.** We will never want for love again. We will know His love.

10. **R.** We will see the face of God and live.

October 1, 1996

Jesus: The Shepherds of Christ Movement will have centers of renewal.

As requested by My Mother, I am asking you to pray the rosary as a continued novena for the Movement. Pray, beginning this day, 27 days in petition, 27 days in thanksgiving for these requests given by My Mother June 17, 1996:

1. For the spread of the rosary, circulation, and publication of these rosary meditations, for the rosary books and children's rosary books, for the rosary Aves and consecrations to be distributed and used by school children.
2. For Our Lady of the Holy Spirit Center.
3. For the Shepherds of Christ centers, for the locations and funds, for the priestly mailing to establish chapters in the churches.

I am requesting that you continually pray this rosary novena from this day forth for these intentions. I am Jesus. I am giving My directions to you, My apostles, in these rosaries from Our Hearts. Please study the rosaries.

I am here and My Mother is here in a special way on the 13th of each month. I am giving to you abundant graces to grow closer to Our Hearts during this rosary. Whenever you use these rosaries, I will give you special graces to help you in this mission, My apostles. Open your hearts and let Me fill your soul with My love. I am alive. I am alive. I am alive, and I live in you. I am Jesus. I come to you with greatest love. Please read the message of Pentecost, 1996 and March 26, 1996 found in this book.

R. For the rosary novena as requested by Jesus and Mary, we pray on the first day the Joyful Mysteries, on the second day the Sorrowful Mysteries, on the third day the Glorious Mysteries. Pray the rosary this way for 27 days in petition, and continue praying the rosary for 27 more days in thanksgiving. Jesus and Mary want us to continue this novena perpetually, 27 days in petition, 27 days in thanksgiving. Please tell all members of the Shepherds of Christ Movement about this request of Jesus and Mary and circulate the above message.

God has entrusted the peace of the world to Mary, she is the Queen of Peace. Mary appeared at Fatima in 1917. Mary's peace plan was given to Lucia as follows:

1. Until a sufficient number of people have consecrated their hearts to the Hearts of Jesus and Mary, we will not have peace in the world.
2. Mary has requested all to pray the daily rosary.
3. We must observe the First Saturday devotion.
4. We must make reparation to the Hearts of Jesus and Mary.

A Final Comment from Jesus

November 12, 1996
Before the Exposed Eucharist

Jesus: My dear, beloved ones, the windows in Our Lady of the Holy Spirit Center are part of the Father's plan.

In praying the rosary, I am asking you to pray to the Holy Spirit and study the pictures in the windows of the mysteries of the rosary. I will reveal to you the insight into the mysteries of My life when you study the pictures. The chart of the position of the windows is important to your study.

Study the Annunciation in reference to the window directly across from it, the Assumption. Study the Visitation in reference to the Descent of the Holy Spirit upon the Apostles. Study the Presentation in reference to the Resurrection and Crucifixion. These pictures were included here at the request of My Mother to help you live lives more like Our lives. Look at the pictures of the Annunciation and the Assumption together. See how Mary's life unfolded according to the Father's plan.

Oh, how I love you. Studying the windows provided here while you pray the rosary will help you to model your lives after Our lives.

This rosary book, *Rosaries from the Hearts of Jesus and Mary*, is very dear to My Most Sacred Heart and the Immaculate Heart of My Mother. Please use this book faithfully. I am giving to you abundant grace to grow more and more in union with Our Hearts when you use this book while praying the rosary.

This is a great Christmas gift for the world. Please be grateful and thank God for these revelations that I give to you. These are insights to take into Our Hearts.

I love you.
Jesus

ABOUT THE ROSARY

Background

The word *rosary* comes from the Latin word *rosarius* which means *crown of roses*. It is a form of prayer arranged to give a litany of praise to God and to honor the Blessed Virgin Mary, the Mother of Jesus, in a special way.

Physically, a complete rosary consists of a series of 150 beads divided into 15 groups or decades of ten beads each. Decades are usually separated from each other by one larger bead and connected to form a continuous loop. Attached to extending from this loop or string are five other beads, two large and three small, and a crucifix. Most rosaries today consist of five decades, one-third of an entire rosary.

Certain prayers are said at each bead of a rosary, a *Hail Mary* on each small bead, an *Our Father* on each large bead, and a *Glory Be* and *O My Jesus* prayer following each decade. The 15 decades are further divided into three groups of five, each group dedicated to a set of five important New Testament events called respectively the Joyful Mysteries, the Sorrowful Mysteries and the Glorious Mysteries. During the rosary, each mystery is first announced, then pondered (contemplated) for a few moments before the recitation of a decade of *Hail Marys*.

Another tool used by the faithful in praying the rosary is to meditate on some aspect of a rosary mystery at each bead, before each *Hail Mary*. Certain meditations in this book follow such a format, with many of them coming through the receiver Rita directly from Jesus and Mary.

The fifteen mysteries of the rosary celebrate important events in the New Testament, events which define great truths of our Christian faith. In the rosary, they are arranged in groups as shown below. For those who pray a five-decade rosary each day, the traditional order for praying the mysteries by day of the week is also shown.

THE JOYFUL MYSTERIES

Said on Mondays and Thursdays and on Sundays from the First Sunday of Advent until Lent

1. The Annunciation to Mary
2. The Visitation of Mary
3. The Nativity of Our Lord
4. The Presentation of the Child Jesus in the Temple
5. The Finding of Jesus in the Temple

THE SORROWFUL MYSTERIES

Said on Tuesdays and Fridays and on the Sundays of Lent

1. The Agony in the Garden
2. The Scourging at the Pillar
3. The Crowning with Thorns
4. The Carrying of the Cross
5. The Crucifixion and Death of Our Lord on the Cross

THE GLORIOUS MYSTERIES

Said on Wednesdays and Saturdays and on Sundays from Easter to Advent

1. The Resurrection of Our Lord
2. The Ascension of Our Lord
3. The Descent of the Holy Spirit on the Apostles and Mary
4. The Assumption of Mary into Heaven
5. The Crowning of Mary Queen of Heaven and Earth

Organization of the Rosary

Strictly speaking, a rosary is a litany of Aves, wave after wave , decades, of Hail Marys directed at Our Lady, begging her intercession on our behalf with God the Father, her Son Jesus and the Holy Spirit. However, the rosary format shown here has been the accepted standard for hundreds of years, with the exception of the *O My Jesus,* or Fatima, prayer which has been added in this century. Most of the individual prayers are ancient indeed, reflecting the glory of the Church from as far back as Our Lord (the *Our Father*), the Gospels (the *Hail Mary*) and the Middle Ages (the *Holy Mary*). Truly a revered and comfortable prayer!

How to Say the Rosary

1. Make the *Sign of the Cross* and say the *Apostles' Creed.*
2. Say the *Our Father.*
3. Say 3 *Hail Marys.*
4. Say the *Glory Be to the Father.*
5. Announce the First Mystery, then say the *Our Father.*
6. Say 10 *Hail Marys.*
7. Say the *Glory Be to the Father.*
8. Say the *O My Jesus.*
9. Announce the Second Mystery, then say the *Our Father,* 10 *Hail Marys, Glory Be* and *O My Jesus.*
10. Announce the Third Mystery, then say the *Our Father,* 10 *Hail Marys, Glory Be* and *O My Jesus.*
11. Announce the Fourth Mystery, then say the *Our Father,* 10 *Hail Marys, Glory Be* and *O My Jesus.*
12. Announce the Fifth Mystery, then say the *Our Father,* 10 *Hail Marys, Glory Be* and *O My Jesus.*
13. Conclude by saying the *Hail Holy Queen.*
14. Make the *Sign of the Cross.*

THE ROSARY PRAYERS

The Sign of the Cross

In the name of the Father and of the Son and of the Holy Spirit. Amen

The Apostles Creed

I believe in God the Father Almighty, Creator of heaven and earth; and in Jesus Christ, His only Son, our Lord; who was conceived by the Holy Spirit, born of the Virgin Mary, suffered under Pontius Pilate, was crucified, died and was buried. He descended into hell; the third day he arose again from the dead; he ascended into heaven; sits at the right hand of God the Father Almighty; from thence he shall come to judge the living and the dead. * I believe in the Holy Spirit, the Holy Catholic Church, the communion of Saints, the forgiveness of sins, the resurrection of the body, and life everlasting. Amen.

Our Father

Our Father, Who art in heaven, hallowed be Thy name. Thy kingdom come, Thy will be done on earth as it is in heaven. * Give us this day our daily bread and forgive us our trespasses as we forgive those who trespass against us. And lead us not into temptation but deliver us from evil. Amen.

Hail Mary

Hail Mary, full of grace, the Lord is with thee; blessed art thou among women, and blessed is the Fruit of thy womb, Jesus. * Holy Mary, Mother of God, pray for us sinners, now and at the hour of our death. Amen.

Glory Be

Glory be to the Father, and to the Son, and to the Holy Spirit. * As it was in the beginning, is now, and ever shall be, world without end. Amen.

O My Jesus

O My Jesus, forgive us our sins, save us from the fires of hell and lead all souls to heaven, especially those who are in most need of Thy mercy.

Hail Holy Queen

Hail, holy Queen, Mother of mercy, our life, our sweetness and our hope. To thee do we cry, poor banished children of Eve. To thee do we send up our sighs, mourning and weeping in this valley of tears. Turn then, most gracious advocate, thine eyes of mercy toward us. And after this, our exile, show unto us the blessed Fruit of thy womb, Jesus, O clement, O loving, O sweet Virgin Mary.

V. Pray for us, O holy Mother of God.

R. That we may be made worthy of the promises of Christ.

Let us pray. O God, whose only begotten Son, by His life, death, and resurrection has purchased for us the rewards of eternal life; grant, we beseech Thee, that meditating upon these mysteries of the most Holy Rosary of the Blessed Virgin Mary, we may imitate what they contain and obtain what they promise, through the same Christ Our Lord. Amen.

Note: When the rosary is said aloud by two or more persons, one person is the leader. He says the first part of the prayer (up to the asterisk *). Everyone else answers by saying the remainder of the prayer. The *O My Jesus* and the *Hail, Holy Queen* are said by all together.

ROSARY SONGS

About the Songs on These Pages

Jesus has written these love songs to you.

On January 26, 1994, Jesus said, "When you live in Me, your life is a song and you play for the world the song of Jesus." (God's Blue Book, Volume 2).

More than nine months later, He gave me *A Song from Jesus*.

On October 7, 1994, Jesus told me to write a song to be sung after Communion for a Mass at Our Lady of the Holy Spirit Center on October 8, 1994. I told Him I couldn't write music. He said, "You will not do it, I will." My daughter and I sat at the piano bench and in five minutes Jesus gave me the words and music to *A Song from Jesus*. This is His love song to you.

In early October, 1994, after Communion, I felt very close to Jesus and went to the Adoration Chapel at Our Lady of the Holy Spirit Center. Jesus was exposed in the monstrance. He told me to write this love song to Him. In fifteen minutes, without a piano, in the silence of the chapel, I wrote the words and the music in my notebook. Later I played the song on the piano—it was so beautiful! This is the love song He wants us to sing to Him, *I Love You, Jesus*.

One night at 10:30 p.m. I was feeling very sad and Jesus told me to go to the piano and write a song. He gave me the song, *Little Child*.

These are love songs from Jesus to us. He wants us to sing them and to hear Him sing them to us. Singing all through the day love songs to Jesus will keep Him in our hearts. When negative thoughts come into our mind, Jesus wants us to sing these love songs. This will keep us connected to the Heart of Jesus. Let us discipline our thoughts by praying the rosary, meditating on the lives of Jesus and Mary, and singing love songs to Jesus. Please circulate these songs to all: to the children, to the elderly, to all His souls.

Songs published in this book are also available on tape from Shepherds of Christ Ministries. Audio and video recordings (and selected messages) available from the Shepherds of Christ Ministries are listed at the rear of this book.

A Song from Jesus

by Rita Ring

Come to My Heart

by Rita Ring

REFRAIN

Let go to Me, My child, I want___ to be___ with you. Come,___ dear child, I love you so much, Come and sur-ren-der to Me.

VERSES 1,2

1. My moth-er calls out___ to you, She wants you to come to her Son, My Heart___ is wait-ing for you. Come and be lost in My love.

2. I want you to dwell in My Heart, I call you to come for My love, I will give you all that you need. Come deep-ly in-to My Heart.

184

Glory, Glory, Glory Lord

by Rita Ring

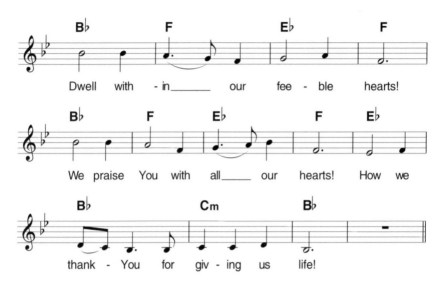

Dwell with - in_____ our fee - ble hearts!

We praise You with all_____ our hearts! How we

thank - You for giv - ing us life!

REFRAIN

We are sin - ners, we need_____ Your grace!

We are wait - ing Your pre - cious life!

Al - le - lu - ia Praise__ the Lord! Je - sus has

ris - en to give us new life!

God's Love

by Rita Ring

1. I love you this___ day; I am your ar - dent
3. The Fa - ther made___ you; No one is just like
4. I want to give you love; You are My spe - cial

love; You wan - der oh so far; Your
you; You are His lit - tle child; He
love; You are My Fa - ther's child; I

soul knows it is hun - gry for on - ly My___
has a plan for you; Live as He wills you
love you oh so dear - ly; Come close and know My

love. 2. You want to know the truth; You
to. 5. The Spir - it knows the way to
love.

look so ma - ny plac-es; You must come to My Heart; Find
lead you to God's love. Be fill - ed with His life; He'll

shel - ter in My Heart; My Heart has all you need.
give you love on fire; You'll know the pow'r of God.

(repeat verse 1)

I Love You Jesus

by Rita Ring

VERSES

1. Oh Burn-ing Heart, Oh Love di - vine, how
2. I can-not say. There are not words to
3. Your ten - der Heart, Oh how it beats for

sweet You are to me. I see the host, I
say what my heart feels. I love You so, I
love of each this day. I want to give You

know You're here to love and care for me.
scarce can breathe when You come in - to me.
all my love, sur - ren - der to - tal - ly.

REFRAIN

I know Your love a lit - tle now, so

dear You are to me. Come give me life, a -

bun - dant life, I thirst to be with Thee.

I Am Your Sacred Heart

by Rita Ring

REFRAIN

In the deep - est re - cess - es of____ My Heart, take__ ref - uge____ from the wind and__ the storm. I will be with you for_____ ev - er - more. I am your Sa - cred Heart.

VERSE 1

1. I am the Way, the Truth and the Life, you will have life in Me. Come, My dear lit - tle chil - dren come, Come and__ live in Me.

Little Child

by Rita Ring

VERSE 1

1. Lit - tle child, lit - tle child, come and rest in My arms. Be with Me, lit - tle child, I want you with Me. You are hurt-ing My lov - ed one, I'm wait - ing for you. Come in - to My Heart now, I love you.

REFRAIN

I am Je - sus, lit - tle child, I have al - ways loved you. From the day you were born, I've been here with you. Do not for - sake Me, I want you to know, lit - tle child, lit - tle child, I love you so!

VERSE 2

2. Let__ go, let__ go, you hold on__ so

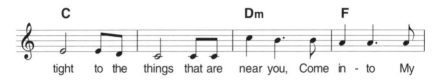

tight to the things that are near you, Come in - to My

light. Your__ heart knows__ long - ing, I am what you

crave. Let go to My pres-ence, I ne - ver go.

Little Baby Hands and Feet

by Rita Ring

REFRAIN

Lit - tle ba - by hands and feet, Loved and cared for by His moth -er;

Sim - e - on fore - told the pain, Je - sus Lord is nailed to the cross.

VERSES 1,2,3

1. Ten - der ba - by lit - tle hands, Mar - y's heart is pierced with a sword;
2. Mar - y is our moth - er too, She will lead us to His — love;
3. Mar - y stood be - neath the cross, How her heart — knows His — Heart;

He has come to give us life, God our Fa - ther gave His Son.
He has giv - en us His life, See Him hang — on the cross.
She watched Him her ten - der Child, Now she takes us to His Heart.

CODA

4. Stand be-side Him know the joy, He has come to bring new life;

Now He ris - es from the dead, Gives us life a - bun - dant life.

My Open Heart

by Rita Ring

My Heart is o - pen and on fire____ for you.

I want____ you to know I'm wait - ing for you.

Come in - to My Heart, I____ long for you.

Do you hear My beat-ing heart? Do you know how near I am?

I am Je - sus lit - tle one, I____ wait for you.

Your Presence Pervades My Soul

by Rita Ring

REFRAIN

Your pres-ence per - vades my soul,___ Your burn-ing love in my heart.___ My heart knows You dear-ly, my soul knows Your pres-ence. Oh Je-sus, I long for Your love.

VERSE 1

1. You are my way, my truth and my life, I for - ev - er want Your pres - ence with - in me.

VERSE 2

2. To You, Oh Lord, I lift up my soul. I give You my life to use as You will.

VERSE 3

3. I want to live for You this day, You
call me to see You in my broth - ers to - day.

VERSE 4

4. I am in your broth - er, I call you to
love___ them. Do not turn Me a - way.

See the Eyes That Look At Mary

by Rita Ring

REFRAIN

See the eyes that look at Mar - y, this ten - der in - fant Child. See this Child's Heart beat so ten - der - ly, the Sav - ior of the world!

Last time to coda

VERSES

1. His__ eyes are gaz - ing stead-i - ly up - on His lov - ing moth-er. She__ sees the Child__ Je - sus, the new-born ba - by here. He__ comes in His en - tire - ty, the Son of God is He.

2. He__ gives us now His bo - dy in the Ho - ly Eu - cha - rist. He__ comes with this in - tense_ love to be so close to us. He__ longs for us to come to Him, His Heart__ waits for us.

Teach Me to Love With Your Heart

by Rita Ring

Other Materials Available
From Shepherds of Christ Ministries

To order materials described below, just fill out the form on the back page of this book (or put required information on a separate sheet). Be sure to fill in the quantity of each desired item. Your donation (checks only; please, no cash through the mail!) is kindly accepted but we emphasize that it is more important for you to have and use the materials than to count dollar value.

Audio Tapes

A1. Love Songs and Messages from the Hearts of Jesus and Mary, October 1, 1995

A2. Shepherds of Christ Associates Spirituality Handbook and Prayer Manual, read by Fr. Edward Carter, S.J.

A3. The Hearts of Jesus and Mary and the Shepherds of Christ, a talk by Fr. Edward Carter, S.J. at St. Ignatius Church, Cincinnati, OH

A4. The Joyful Mysteries, Rosary meditations given on February 1, 1995

A5. The Sorrowful Mysteries, Rosary meditations given on March 17, 1995

A6. The Sorrowful Mysteries, Rosary received during a Shepherds of Christ prayer meeting on July 11, 1995

A7. The Glorious Mysteries, Rosary meditations given on February 22, 1995

A8. Tell My People, Messages from Jesus and Mary for the world; Messages received and read by Fr. Carter

A9. Songs and Messages from the Hearts of Jesus and Mary, October 24, 1995

A10. The Sorrowful Mysteries, Rosary meditations given on July 28, 1995

A11. The Glorious Mysteries, Rosary meditations concerning the children of the world, July 15, 1995

A12. Children's Joyful Mysteries and Prayer Manual Prayers, Rosary Meditations given on December 25, 1994
Rosary and prayers recited by children.

A13. Choose Life, Songs and Messages, November 21, 1995

A14. Prayer Manual of the Shepherds of Christ Associates, Read by Father Edward Carter, S.J.

A15. The Hearts of Jesus and Mary, Talk given by Fr. Edward J. Carter, S. J. at Denver, CO, January 4, 1996
This talk by Fr. Carter is about the Fatima message and its connection to the Shepherds of Christ Movement.

A16. The Glorious Mysteries, Rosary meditations given on May 11, 1996 in Toledo, Ohio

LIVE rosaries are rosaries which you are hearing the actual tape as the rosary was received.

A17. The Sorrowful Mysteries, Rosary meditations given on September 10, 1996 **LIVE**

A18. The Glorious Mysteries, Rosary meditations given on October 13, 1996 **LIVE**

A19. The Sorrowful Mysteries, Rosary meditations given on November 13, 1996 **LIVE**

A20. Mary's Message, December 12, 1996, Feast of Our Lady of Guadeloupe

A21. The Joyful Mysteries, Rosary meditations given on December 13, 1996 **LIVE**

A22. The Joyful Mysteries, Rosary meditations given on January 13, 1997 **LIVE**

A23. The Sorrowful Mysteries, Rosary meditations given on February 13, 1997 **LIVE**

A24. The Sorrowful Mysteries, Rosary meditations *without messages* given on August 20, 1996

A25. Songs from Jesus

A26. Daily Prayers

A27. The Joyful Mysteries, Rosary meditations given on March 30, 1995

A28. 15 Decade Rosary, Rosary is recited by Fr. Edward Carter, S. J., John Weickert and Rita Ring. There are no meditations for any of the decades.

A29. Nursing Home Tape: Messages from Jesus and Mary

A30. Messages from God's Blue Book II

A31. Hourly Novena and Jesus, I Want to be with You, Infant of Prague Novena and a song

A32. Shepherds of Christ Priestly Newsletter Issue 2, 1998

A33. Shepherds of Christ Priestly Newsletter Issue 3, 1998

A34. Shepherds of Christ Priestly Newsletter Issue 4, 1998

A35. Daily Messages from Florida, Volume I, July 8-27, 1998

A36. Daily Messages from Florida, Volume II, July 28 - August 1998

A37. Daily Messages from Florida, Volume III

A38. The Sorrowful Mysteries, March 21, 1995, from Florida

A39. The Glorious Mysteries, April 16, 1995, from Florida

A40. Children's Joyful Mysteries, March 20, 1997 & Glorious Mysteries, April 25, 1996, from Florida

A42. The Sorrowful Mysteries, April 21, 1995 & Glorious Mysteries, July 15, 1995, from Florida

Rosary Aves are short meditations for the rosary with the imprimatur for schools.

A43. Joyful and Sorrowful Rosary Aves, without messages

A44. Glorious Rosary Aves, Stations of the Cross, 7 Sorrows, without messages

Video Tapes

V1. The Hearts of Jesus and Mary, talk given by Fr. Edward J. Carter S. J. at Denver, Colorado, January 4, 1996
This talk by Fr. Carter is about the Fatima message and it's connection to the Shepherds of Christ Movement. He talks about consecrating our hearts to the Hearts of Jesus and Mary and about having a close union with Jesus.

V2. Messages from Jesus, an interview with Rita Ring, April 17, 1994
Rita sings songs and reads messages from *God's Blue Book*, Volume 1.
These are messages about Jesus' love for us, messages about visiting Jesus
in the tabernacle. Rita tells how she started receiving messages.

V3. A Mist Around Mary, September 5, 1995
Mary appeared to Rita almost every day from July 5, 1994 until
September 5, 1995 at Our Lady of the Holy Spirit Center in Norwood,
Ohio. A video taken at the September 5 rosary revealed a pink mist over
the statue during key meditations of the rosary. This video is part of a
"live" rosary (a "live" rosary is one recorded as Rita Ring receives messages from Jesus and Mary). Most rosaries last about one hour. They are
taped and these meditations and messages are then transcribed from tape.
Mary has requested that we circulate this video of the mist and the messages given on that date, messages Jesus and Mary want you to hear.

V4. Mary's Message and Witnesses given in Clearwater, Florida

Books

B1. God's Blue Book, Volume 1, by Rita Ring. Lessons from Jesus about living in and loving Him in our times. Remarkable insights into appreciating
Our Lord in the Blessed Sacrament and in the tabernacle. Private dialogues
between God and a chosen one.

B2. God's Blue Book, Volume 2.

B3. God's Blue Book, Volume 3.

B4. Tell My People. Messages given to Father Edward J. Carter, S.J. from
Jesus and Mary. Messages, reflections and prayers for growing in holiness
through devotion to the Immaculate Heart of Mary and the Sacred Heart of
Jesus.

B5. Mother at My Side, by Father Edward Carter, S.J. An easy to read look at
Mary's role in our lives.

B6. The Spirituality of Fatima and Medjugorje, by Father Edward J. Carter,
S.J. The key idea of this book is: "...We see the profound link, the pro-
found point of convergence between the spirituality of Fatima and
Medjugorje. It is the ongoing conversion based on consecration to the
Sacred Heart and to the Immaculate Heart..." (page 43 of the text)

B7. Rosary Meditations for Parents and Children, by Rita Ring. Short
meditations (without messages) for both parents and children to be used
when praying the rosary. These meditations will help all to know the lives
of Jesus and Mary alive in their hearts.

B8. Mass Book, by Rita Ring. Journal entries of a chosen soul concerning the
events during the Holy Sacrifice of the Mass. These entries help to lead
other souls deeply into the Heart of Christ during the Mass.

B9. Apostles Manual, (440 pages) A manual for Apostles in the Shepherds of
Christ Movement.

Order Form

In the space provided, write in the quantity of the desired item(s) to be shipped. Don't forget to print clearly your own name and address to assure shipping accuracy.

Audio Tapes:

___ A1	___ A7	___ A13	___ A19	___ A25	___ A31	___ A37	___ A43
___ A2	___ A8	___ A14	___ A20	___ A26	___ A32	___ A38	___ A44
___ A3	___ A9	___ A15	___ A21	___ A27	___ A33	___ A39	
___ A4	___ A10	___ A16	___ A22	___ A28	___ A34	___ A40	
___ A5	___ A11	___ A17	___ A23	___ A29	___ A35	___ A41	
___ A6	___ A12	___ A18	___ A24	___ A30	___ A36	___ A42	

Video Tapes:

___ V1 ___ V2 ___ V3 ___ V4

Books:

___ B1 ($5.00*)	___ B4 ($4.00*)	___ B7 ($5.00*)
___ B2 ($5.00*)	___ B5 ($6.00*)	___ B8 ($7.00)
___ B3 ($5.00*)	___ B6 ($6.00*)	___ B9 ($7.50)

*Suggested donation price each.

There are many books and tapes available on a brochure.

To receive the books, tapes, and more information call or write:

Phone (Toll Free) 1-888-211-3041 or 513-932-4451.
Fax No. 513-932-6791.
Internet: http://www.shepherds-of-christ.org.
Email: Info@shepherds-of-christ.org.

Send materials to:

Name _____

Address _____

City _____ State _____ Zip _____

Enclosed Donation: ___ $200 ___ $100 ___ $50 _____ Other

Send order to:

Shepherds of Christ Ministries • P.O. Box 193 • Morrow, OH 45152

Shepherds of Christ Ministries is a non-profit organization which supports its works entirely on donations. We appreciate your honoring our regeneration costs according to your means. When ordering books directly from the Ministries, please add $1.50 for each book ($5.00 outside of North America), total mailing cost not to exceed $10.00 per order ($20.00 outside of North America). For audio tapes, add $1.00 for every 5 tapes. For video tapes, add $2.00 per tape.